BOOK 4

WHAT JESUS TAUGHT ABOUT . . .

BOOK 4

What Jesus Taught About . . .

Love, Marriage and Divorce,
Women, Children

HERBERT LOCKYER

VICTORY PRESS
EASTBOURNE

Published by arrangement with Harper and Row
Publishers, Inc., New York.

First British edition 1977

ISBN 0 85476 266 3

Printed in Great Britain for Kingsway
Publications Ltd., Lottbridge Drove,
Eastbourne, E. Sussex, BN23 6NT,
by Fletcher & Son Ltd, Norwich.

Contents

Introduction

Never since God endowed the first man with the power of speech has any human uttered more wonderful words than those leaving the holy lips of Jesus in the days of his flesh. His were not only "Thoughts that breathe, and words that burn," but mighty words that were to shape the destinies of men and nations. Down the ages multitudes have "wondered at the gracious words which proceeded out of his mouth" (Luke 4:22). The world at large agrees with the commendation of those Roman officers that "Never man spake like this man" (John 7:46).

The immediate spontaneous reaction to his oral ministry was remarkable. Interest in his preaching and teaching was widespread, crowds coming from every quarter to hear him (Mark 1:45). How the people hung on his words (Luke 19:48)! On one occasion clamor for his teaching drove him into a boat for a pulpit. No wonder they "marveled at his words of charm"—*charm* and *beautiful* being translated for "gracious" by some commentators (Luke 4:22). Jesus could say, "Out of the abundance of the heart the mouth speaketh"

(Matt. 12:34; Luke 6:45). And what a bountiful heart his own words reveal!

People flocked to him because his language was easy and straightforward. He stuck to plain words the common people could easily understand. He never spoke of God in nebulous terms as the "Great First Cause," or any other vague abstract, but as "your heavenly Father." His was no scholastic vocabulary forcing him to speak over the heads of his listeners. "I seek divine simplicity in him who handles things divine." His words came straight from his inmost being, natural and inevitable, proof of deity and humanity, and they reacted with the life that brought them forth, consequently transfiguring the lives of many who heard him teach.

—1—

About Love

That the fragrance of *love* permeates the four Gospels is evident from the fact that such an emotion is mentioned over eighty times, principally by Jesus, God's much-loved Son. As H. H. Halley expresses it in his valuable *Bible Handbook:*

> Love is the premier teaching of Christianity, and an undying expression of Jesus' doctrine. It is more potent for the building of the Church than any, or all, of the various manifestations of God's power. Love is the Church's most effective weapon, without which all the various gifts of the Spirit are of no avail. Love is the essence of God's nature, as well as the perfection of human character. Love is the most powerful, ultimate force in the Universe.

Because of the paramount importance of love, then, we need to understand all that Jesus taught of its exercise toward himself, God, and man. In passing, it is fitting to observe that as all the three persons of the godhead are coequal in all of their manifested attributes and virtues, all three share in the affection and in the desire for possession and companionship the term *love* suggests. *God the Father* is love in its highest form and reality

(John 3:16). *God the Son* reflected the essence of the Father (John 14:21). *God the Holy Spirit* produces in our hearts the fruit of love (Rom 5:5; Gal. 5:22). James testifies to a *jealous yearning* in the Holy Spirit over Christians infected with "love of the world" (James 4:5; see Eph. 4:13).

Love, in its English form, as found in our modern Bible represents several different Greek words, and it is necessary to distinguish the various shades of meaning.

Eros. Running through Greek philosophy and culture is this term indicating love or desire from the human side and romantic attachment with sexual overtones. The New Testament, however, never uses this word for *love.*

Philia is a word standing for love between friends. *Philcō* means to be a friend and is used in this way some fourteen times in the Gospels. The American city, Philadelphia, means the City of Brotherly Love. This term indicates a reasoning, discriminating attachment, founded in the conviction that its object is worthy of esteem, or entitled to it on account of benefits bestowed. It emphasizes the *intelligent* element of love. The Greek *Philia* usually appears, then, in the context of human love.

Agapē. From *Agapaō,* this term is used more often in the Gospels than any other for *love.* It occurs over fifty times, with over thirty of these being found in John's Gospel. This term, as well as the others above, are all from the same Hebrew word for love, namely *Aheh,* which has as many shades of meaning as the English word *love. Agapē* signifies primarily a voluntary, active affection and comes from the LXX (the Septuagint, earliest

Greek translation of the Old Testament by seventy translators) into the New Testament in the deeper sense of spiritual affection, the love that links God and man and unites soul and soul in the divine communion. This word represents a warmer, more instinctive sentiment, more closely allied to feeling and implying more passion. It emphasizes the *affectional* element of love. It denotes religious love, the love of God to man and man to God, or man to man under God's covenant (Lev. 19:18). Archbishop Trench speaks of it as "a word born in the bosom of revealed religion." This love, suffused with religion, like *Philia,* implies reciprocity and fellowship—if not existing, then desired and sought.

The epithet *beloved,* found in "Well-Beloved," "Dearly Beloved," and "My Beloved," is a derivative of *Agapē* and is used of Christ by God—of Christians, as dear to God, of Christians, as dear to fellow believers or "the brethren." Let us now endeavor to classify the various features of *love* as taught by the Master.

— 2 —

Divine Love

Under this section we outline what the four Gospels teach about God and love and about Christ and love.

GOD AND LOVE

Love is not one of God's majestic attributes but the essence of his being. "God *is* love" (1 John 4:8, 16); the repetition indicates divine emphasis. "Love is of God" since "God is love." Love comes from him because it is absolutely in him. God is love's prime fountain, and therefore *love* gives the best conception we can form of his nature. With all his wisdom, man will never be able to plumb the depths of phrases like "God so loved" (John 3:16) and "The love of God" (John 5:42; Luke 11:42).

The character of God as "Jehovah" and as the "Holy One of Israel" gives his love its qualities of purity, intensity, selflessness, fidelity, and mercy. Reciprocal love should call forth like qualities in his people. But when his love was affronted, it could break into grief, anger, wrath, and threatening against the wanton and faithless (Ps. 78:40; Isa. 63:9)— an aspect of love the loving Son of God also revealed.

God's love for Christ. John, the apostle of love, records more than any other New Testament writer the various aspects of divine love. Not only was God's love exhibited in Christ, it was likewise showered upon him who came as the Son of his love, as Jesus himself emphasized. "The Father loveth the Son" and consequently "sheweth him all things that he himself doeth" (John 5:20).

Revelation came as the result of a blissful relationship. Further, because of his willing sacrifice, Jesus was loved of God: "Therefore doth my Father love me, *because* I lay down my life, that I might take it again" (John 10:17). Then, on his own confession, Jesus reflected the love God had toward him: "As the Father hath loved me, so have I loved you" (John 15:9).

That God wants the world to know about his love for his well-beloved Son (Matt. 3:17) is evident from the High Priestly Prayer: "That the world may know that thou . . . hast loved me" (John 17:23). Loved by God before the foundation of the world, Jesus desired that the same eternal love borne him by the Father might be manifested toward those given him by the Father: "That the love wherewith thou hast loved me may be in them, and I in them" (John 17:24, 26). Because of his love for his Son, God made him the executive of the godhead: "The Father loveth the Son, and hath given all things into his hand."

This perfect form of love bestowed upon the Son by the Father was not merely an affectionate sentiment, but implied an intelligent discernment of the Son as one worthy of such love and therefore entitled to all the divine benefits bestowed upon him.

God's love for all men. If it is possible for one text in the Bible to be greater than another, surely John 3:16—the gospel in a nutshell—is the greatest verse in the Bible: "God so loved the world"—thankless and evil though it is (Luke 6:35). The perfection of God's character lies in his love heaped upon the worst and seeking out those most alienated from him (Matt. 5:48; Luke 15). By the term *would* we are not to understand the beautiful world in which we live, and which God pronounced *good* after he had created it, but a world of sinners ruined by the Fall. Bring forth the most wretched sinner it is possible to find, who cannot fall any deeper into sin, and I will show you something deeper still—the deep, bottomless abyss of God's love.

Paul says that God *commended* this universal love of his while men were adamantly estranged from him. "God commendeth his love toward us, in that, while we were yet sinners, Christ died for us"—the evidence of such love. The word *commend* carries with it the idea of "recommendation" or establishment. So Phillips translates it, "The proof of God's amazing love is this: that it was *while we were sinners* that Christ died for us" (Rom. 5:8). The love, then, that God "commends" subsisted in him apart from and anterior to the proof of the cross; it actuates all his dealings with mankind—in creation, providence, and moral discipline (Matt. 5:45; 6:23–34; 10:29; see James 1:17; 1 Pet. 4:19). Since the objects of God's love are pitiable, sinners exceedingly, his redeeming love is manifested in *mercy,* in which love predominates (Luke 1:50; see Eph. 2:4; Titus 3:5).

God's love for the disciples. The previous aspect of divine love was universal and general; this feature is particular and personal. All sinners saved by grace are equally loved by the Father and the Son. That the Father has a peculiar love for the saints for two reasons is evident from the teaching of his Son. "The Father himself loveth you, because ye have *loved me,* and *have believed* that I came out from God" (John 16:27). "That the world may know that thou . . . hast loved them" (John 17:23).

While there may be a direct application of these utterances to the first disciples of Jesus, they are not limited to them but apply to saints of all ages —to the church he said he would build. This is the love of God in Christ Jesus from which we can never be separated (Rom. 8:35, 39)—passages in which Paul emphasizes the double love, making the believer forever secure.

> Loved in the past of yesterday,
> And all along our future way,
> And in the present of today,
> Forever loved.

(The reader will refer to the section, "About God," Vol. I, for further material on the different features of his love.)

God commands men to love him. In his answer to his carping critics, the Pharisees, Jesus informed them that the first and great commandment in the Law was, "Thou *shalt* love the Lord thy God with all thy heart, and with all thy soul, and with all thy mind" (Matt. 22:37). Paul also declared that men are bidden to love God (1 Cor. 8:1–6).

To those who obey the divine command and truly love God, "all things work together for good" (Rom. 8:28). Jesus did not invent the two commandments about love in his reply to the question; he was simply quoting from the Law of Moses (Lev. 19:18; Deut. 6:5). He stamped the ancient law of love with fresh honor and authority and "elevated it to shine forever as the sun and the moon of the firmament of duty."

Love to God, holding a prominent place in Scripture and especially in the teaching of Jesus, is not something we can please ourselves about but constitutes obedience to a positive command, "Thou shalt love the Lord thy God." Professor Stalker draws attention to a well-known saying of the English statesman, William Pitt. Chancing to visit a church in which a sermon had been preached by one of the apostles of the Evangelical Revival, the doctrines of which were then only beginning to be heard of, Pitt bounced out at the close of the service, exclaiming in high tones, "Why, that fellow expects us to love God!" But such love is not only expected, but commanded, and anyone refusing to love God is lacking in one of the functions of a complete humanity.

Further, the love demanded is not confined to an emotional feeling but should be a supreme passion according to the sweeping declaration of Jesus when he adopted the Mosaic law of love as his own. God must be loved with:

"All thy heart"—the central part out of which are the issues of life.

"All thy soul"—my soul is my self and includes all self action.

"All thy strength"—this involves the will and means moral and physical strength.

"All thy mind"—this part of our human nature is the intellect with all its power to think and plan.

Such language of psychology claims for God the affection of human nature in all its extent and in all its intensity.

Break through my nature, mighty heavenly Love,
  Clear every avenue of thought and brain,
Flood my affections, purify my will,
  Let nothing but Thine own pure life remain.

CHRIST AND LOVE

The love he taught was not a sentiment but a principle, and likewise the substance of his teaching. It is both comforting and assuring that we are equally loved by the Father and the Son. The appeal of Mary and Martha to Jesus concerning their brother Lazarus brought an immediate response. "Behold, he whom thou lovest is sick" (John 11:3). "Jesus loved Martha, and her sister, and Lazarus" (John 11:5). "Then said the Jews, Behold how he loved him" (John 11:36). The tear-stained face of Jesus as he stood at the graveside testified to his deep love for the friend he raised again from the dead. Thus, he was not the mere channel of his Father's love; Jesus shared in it infinitely so much so that *the love of God* is seen in *the love of Christ* (John 10:11–15; 13:1, 34; 14:21; see Rom. 8:35, 39; Rev. 1:5).

Christ loves God. The eternal love of Jesus for the Father (John 17:4) is seen in his unceasing obedience to the divine will, "I do always the things that please my Father." Love delights in obedience and reveals itself in service and sacrifice (John 14:21). "I love the Father" (John 14:31). "I . . . abide in his love" (John 15:10).

From the dateless past Jesus had been the well-beloved Son of God, and such a close-knit bond was the Master's stay in the dark and lonely hours of his sojourn among men. Those short, swift cries of his, wrung from him in his agony, that seemed to pierce the silent heaven like the sob of a heart grief had broken, were personal, came straight from him, and went straight to his Father, whom he had loved from before the beginning of time.

While we have no biblical record of the first thirty years of the life of Jesus among men, apart from a brief glimpse when he was twelve years of age, all through this long period, as well as during his short span of ministry, he manifested a love to God, equal to any service, making obedience, however seemingly hard, spontaneous. He likewise evidenced a love to man equal to any sacrifice, able with a truly divine freedom to give himself for the life of the world, which he did. As the sons of God through grace, may ours be the undying heart-confession—*I love the Father.*

Christ loved his disciples. Professor Stalker reminds us that the only way of making a commandment of love easier is by exhibiting the object of love in a more attractive light. The great contribution of Jesus to this primary duty of morality was that he made God more lovable than he had ever appeared before, especially in the frequent declarations of his love for his chosen disciples. "He that loveth me shall be loved of my Father, and *I* will love him" (John 14:21). "As the Father hath loved me, so have I loved you; continue ye in my love" (John 15:9, 10).

Because Christ loved the church he brought into being by his death, his express wish is that those whom he loves should be with him where he is (John 14:3; 17:24). Further, in the truth of the fatherhood of God about which Jesus fully instructed his disciples, there is resident the thought of divine love for them. Jesus habitually called God *my Father;* when he denominated God when speaking to his disciples, he called him *your Father* and taught them to pray to him as *our Father.* Such fatherhood was the culminating expression in the revelation for the love of God, a love which, in turn, Jesus manifested toward those given him of the Father.

One of the most impressive affirmations of the love Jesus bore for his disciples is that given by John. "Having loved his own which were in the world, he loved them unto the end [or, *to the uttermost*]" (John 13:1).

As the hymnist expresses it,

> There is no love like the love of Jesus—
> Never to fade or fall.

What is the implication of the phrase, "He loved them unto the end"? Godet translates it, "He perfectly testified unto them all his love" and comments that "unto the end" means *to the utmost, to make an end of it.* John's assuring word does not signify that Jesus *did not cease* to love his own up to the moment when he died for them. Divine love is eternal and cannot, therefore, cease. This phrase signifies therefore the manifestation of his love even to its complete outpouring, in a way to exhaust it, in some sort.

What is true of the Father is likewise true of his Son: "I have loved thee with an everlasting love:

therefore with lovingkindness have I drawn thee" (Jer. 31:3). George Matheson gave us the heart-moving hymn, "O Love, That Wilt Not Let Me Go." Paul, who gave us the paradox of knowing the unknowable love of Christ—a love making us more than conquerors—also confirms that nobody and nothing can ever separate us from the love of the Father and the Son (Rom. 8:35, 39).

Loved with everlasting love,
  Led by grace that love to know;
Spirit, breathing from above,
  Thou hast taught me it is so.

Christ loves the individual. The aspect of love just considered is of a particular nature—*his own.* But as we have already indicated, the love of Jesus was also personal, as many proved who crossed his pathway. For instance, there was the rich young ruler: "Jesus beholding him loved him" (Mark 10:21). Behold how he loved Lazarus" (John 11:3, 5, 36). "Now there was leaning on Jesus' bosom, one of his disciples, whom Jesus loved" (John 13:23).

Three times over we have the phrase "the disciple whom Jesus loved" (John 13:23; 20:2; 21:20). That this disciple was John himself is proven by his own statement, "This is the disciple which testifieth of these things" (John 21:24). With all due reticence and reverence, this disciple, who leaned on the bosom of Jesus, did not mention his name. As Godet puts it, if John designates himself by this paraphrase—the Disciple whom Jesus loved—it is precisely from humility that he avoids declaring his name, but with the feeling of the infinite condescension of him who had designed to treat him, during his earthly existence, as *his friend.*

When Jesus focused his love upon an individual, it was because of qualities his deep look discovered in them—qualities and virtues he knew his love was able to enrich and ennoble. The marvel and mystery of grace is that each of us, as the redeemed of the Lord, is the object and recipient of his love. Paul, who reveled in preaching and writing about the love of Jesus, experienced its personal aspect, "The Son of God, who loved *me,* and gave himself for *me*" (Gal. 2:20).

It passeth knowledge, that dear love of Thine,
My Saviour, Jesus; yet this soul of mine
Would of Thy love, in all its breadth and length,
Its height and depths, its everlasting strength,
Know more and more.

Christ manifested his love by the cross. The Master had much to say about the fact and manner of his death at Calvary (John 3:14). "Greater love hath no man than this, that a man lay down his life for his friends. *Ye are my friends*" (John 15:13, 14). It is undoubtedly a greater proof of love when one is willing to sacrifice his life for his enemies, which Jesus did, seeing "he died for the ungodly." While we were yet sinners, Jesus laid down his life for us, and such sacrificial love founded a new empire of love resulting in a regime and fashion of life hitherto unknown. The wondrous love, willing to bleed and die, binds the redeemed to the service of the Redeemer and transforms them into witnesses of God's covenant of grace in Jesus made with mankind (Matt. 10:4; Mark 16:15; 1 John 2:2).

Inscribed upon the Cross we see,
In shining letters—*God is Love.*

The Christian church of apostolic times celebrated the *Agapē*, or Love Feast, which included the Lord's Supper, and at which there was the loving remembrance of the broken body and outpoured blood of Jesus for man's salvation. Saints still gather for the feast, keeping thereby "the memory adored."

His body broken in our stead
Is seen, in this memorial bread,
And so our feeble love is fed
  Until He comes.

The drop of His dread agony,
His life-blood shed for us, we see;
The wine shall tell the mystery
  Until He come.

Christ expects men to love him and God. Love toward God and Christ is the heart's response to the Father's love exhibited in Christ (1 John 4:19) and is a love resulting from faith. "If a man love me, he will keep my words" (John 14:23). "Continue ye in my love . . . Abide in his love" (John 15:9–10). "Lovest thou me more than these" (John 21:15–17)?

In his unique conversation with Peter, Jesus sought to restore him to his old position as chief of the apostles, an office he had lost by his denial. The connection between his threefold denial of Jesus and his threefold affirmation of love for Jesus is somewhat striking. There was a sense in which this threefold profession of his love for the one he had denied effaced the threefold strain he had brought upon himself. Jesus asked Peter whether he loved him "more than these," meaning more than the other disciples over whom he had felt superiority (Matt. 26:33; Mark 14:29). The first question of Jesus seems to convey a gentle rebuke for Peter's former extravagant professions.

Jesus used the more dignified, really the nobler, word for *love*—to love in the higher and spiritual sense of the word, love with the love of reverence. Peter, however, in the ardor of his affection, felt this to be the colder word for *love* and so substituted the warmer, more affectionate term of loving in the sense of personal attachment. He thinks that he can without presumption ascribe to himself this latter feeling; and yet he does not do it without expressing distrust of himself and without seeking the guaranty of the testimony of his heart to which he does not dare to trust any longer in the infallible knowledge of the hearts of men, which he now attributes to his Master.

The love Jesus asks of us, and the love he bears toward us, renovates and purifies the heart, inspires a constant self-devotion to the feeding of his sheep and lambs, and makes the perfect vision of God the object of fervent anticipation (John 14:23; 17:24; 1 John 1:1–3; 4:10). May we be saved from the rebuke Jesus administered to the church at Ephesus for having left their "first love" (Rev. 2:4).

> Shall I not yield to that constraining power?
> Shall I not say, O tide of Love, flow in?
> My God, Thy gentleness hath conquered me,
> Life cannot be as it hath hither been.

Christ taught that love is the sum and substance of the Law. It is clear from his teaching on *love* that it is by such that the Law can be truly kept. It is only as man loves God and his fellow-men that we can fulfill the ancient command. "Love is the fulfilling of the law," Paul affirms. Of old, God showed mercy unto thousands who loved him and kept his commandments (Exod. 20:6), a revelation Jesus emphasizes: "Thou shalt love the Lord thy God" (Matt. 22:37, 38; Luke 10:27). Because God is the source of love, we love him (1 John 4:19). Ancient Israel sinned against divine love, broke the covenant, transgressed the Law; yet love flowed on, ever seeking to bring sinners to share once again in the care of the divine heart.

"How shall I give thee up, Ephraim" (Hos. 11:8)? His banner of love was ever over God's erring children. The many waters of rejection could not quench such pursuing love. In his love and pity, he sought to redeem them, for his love would not let them go.

Coming to the New Testament, we find the self-expressed righteous Pharisees, confident in the security of their own relation to Jehovah, but who deemed publicans and sinners, Samaritans and Gentiles, as being outside of the ancient covenant of love and mercy. But it was against this dark background that Jesus taught the fatherly love of God—a love embracing all without distinction and which could not be dissolved by the ill-doing of its objects. It was because of his own love, so often spurned, that he died for the ungodly. Well might John Milton exclaim:

> O unexampled love!
> Love nowhere to be found less than Divine!

Because, then, of the preeminence of love as proclaimed by Jesus, may we be found resting in, and responding to, and reciprocating such external love, even as Toplady exhorts us:

> Loved of my God, for Him again
> With love intense I burn!—
> Chosen of Thee ere time began,
> I choose Thee in return!

—3—

Human Love

Jowett of Balliol would have us remember that "The love of Christ is the conducting medium to the love of all mankind." It is like the inspiration of our love to God, as well as to man. From the teaching of Jesus we learn that the spring of human love flows out in four directions, namely, in love for God, in the family circle, among believers, and toward our neighbor.

MAN'S LOVE FOR GOD

Attention has been drawn to this feature of human love. It has been pointed out that the overwhelming preponderance of the New Testament usage is in favor of the essential unity of the love *(agapē)* which God manifests to his creation and the love *(agapē)* which Christians are to have for God and for one another. God merits and desires the love of man (1 John 4:19). All pure forms of earthly love point upward to features of the divine love. In the first place, however, the great and incomprehensible in the divine being kindles all the earthly fires of true love. How blessed we are if found among the ardent "lovers of God"!

When Jesus described the end-time period of the Gentile age, he said that one characteristic feature would be that the love of many would wax cold (Matt. 24:12). Coldness certainly sums up the witness of the church today in love for God, for his truth, and for his cause. It is hard in these increasingly sinful times to walk close with God and keep our love for him and all that is dear to him fresh, warm, and active. May grace be ours to emulate the aspiration of Madam Guyon!

> Why have I not a thousand thousand hearts,
>   Lord of my Soul! that they might all be Thine!
> If Thou approve—the zeal Thy smile imparts,
>   How should it ever fail! Can such a fire decline?
> Love, pure and holy, is a deathless fire,—
>   Its object heavenly;—it must ever blaze!
> Eternal Love a God must needs inspire,
>   When once He wins the heart, and fits it for His praise.

LOVE IN THE FAMILY CIRCLE

Jesus was born into and grew up in the loving atmosphere of a godly home and came to experience the close, intimate love between parents and children making a home heaven's twin sister. Yet he made it clear that such human love must be subservient to love for him. "He that loveth father or mother more than me is not worthy of me: and he that loveth son or daughter more than me is not worthy of me" (Matt. 10:37). In all things, even in the realm of family love, he must have the preeminence. These words of Jesus in which he claims our best are remarkable in that he demands for himself a higher affection than any parent or any child can claim. If we would be worthy of being his disciple, we must love him best of all because he loves us more dearly than all. There is beauty all around, not only when there is love at home, but more especially, if Jesus is Lord in the home.

Matthew's "loveth more" softens the harsher expression of Luke's "hateth not" (Luke 14:26). Bible readers are sometimes perplexed over the phrase, "Hateth not his father and mother, and wife and children and brethren, and sisters." What must be borne in mind is that the word *hate* does not mean to hate in the sense in which we use the word today, namely, as expression of intense aversion or to dislike or abhor exceedingly. Such a command to hate in this way would be utterly foreign to the benign character of Jesus and contrary to the tenor of his teaching on *love.*

It will be recalled that Jacob is said to have *hated* Leah (Gen. 29:31), that is, he loved her less than Rachel. "He loved also Rachel more than Leah" (Gen. 29:30), meaning that she had the preeminent place in her husband's affection. This explanation is akin to the reported sayings of Jesus as to true discipleship in which "loving more" takes the place of the yet stronger form of "not hating." What Jesus asked of his own was nothing less than the heart, and that cannot be given by halves. The condition, hard though it may seem, implies that where two affections come into collision, the weaker must give way; and though the man may not and ought not to cease to love, yet he must act as if he hated—disobey, and, it may be, desert—those to whom he is bound by natural ties, that he may obey the higher supernatural calling. Loving Jesus more never means loving our dear ones less. The spiritual affection enriches natural affection.

LOVE AMONG BELIEVERS

Another badge of true and effective discipleship is love among ourselves as fellow believers. If sinners love fellow sinners, as Jesus indicated (Luke 6:33, 34), saints should love, not only fellow saints, but their enemies (Luke 6:35) and "the evil" (Matt. 5:43–48).

"By this—that ye also love one another—shall all men know that ye are my disciples" (John 13:34, 35). John, the apostle of love, extends the teaching of Jesus on *love* and gives us the final and complete New Testament doctrine of such a theme. The apostle saw the love of God perfected in those who "love one another" and thus "keep God's commands" from whose soul accordingly "fear" is "cast out." As they "abide" wholly in the realm of love that is constituted by the one loving Spirit dwelling in their hearts, they are "perfected unto one," even as Christ is "one" with the Father by virtue of the love subsisting eternally between them, which is love's prime fountain (Matt. 3:17; John 17:21–26; 1 John 2:5; 3:24; 4:11–21).

We are liars if we profess to love God yet hate a brother we can see. If we cannot love him, how can we love God whom we cannot see (1 John 4:20)? In the early days of the church, when the disciples had a deeper concern for each other, the surrounding heathen would admiringly say, "See how these Christians love one another!" Now the same phrase is uttered with bitter sarcasm by the world that sees the feuds, unhappy divisions, and acrimony among those who profess to be lovers of God. Jesus said that to love one another as he has loved us, was a "new commandment." Would that a loveless church could be found obeying it (see Rom. 12:10, 13–16)!

Beloved, let us love:
  Love is of God;
In God alone hath love
  Its true abode.

Beloved, let us love;
  For they who love,
They only are His sons,
  Born from above.

LOVE TOWARD OUR NEIGHBOR

Jesus lifted "the second great commandment," as he called it—"Thou shalt love thy neighbour as thyself"—right out of the Book of Leviticus and stamped it with his imprimatur (Lev. 19:18; Luke 10:27). The lawyer asked Jesus, "Who is my neighbour?" and he received a new idea as to the identity of his neighbor and of neighborly conduct. *Who is your neighbor?* Is he the one who lives next door to you or across the street? Is he the one of the same nation and race as yourself? Where do we come upon those who are no longer our neighbors?

Among the best-known and best-loved parables of Jesus are the parable of the lost son (Luke 15) and the parable of the good Samaritan (Luke 10:30–37). The first parable deals primarily with the relationship of man to God, while the second emphasizes man's relationship with his fellow-man. Man is "not an island by himself, but a part of the main continent of humanity," as the lawyer learned from Jesus' illustration of who his neighbor was. The Samaritan journeying from Jerusalem to Jericho found another traveler who had been robbed and brutally mugged on the roadside and bestowed upon him every care and attention. As a true neighbor he showed mercy upon the half-dead man.

Does not this superb illustration teach that a man's neighbor is a man in distress and need, no matter of what nation or race or color he may be? This is the loving mercy that God delights to show to man and Jesus taught men to show to one another (see Rom. 12:20, 21). Our neighbor, then, is the one we meet in need and whom it is in our power to help. Chief among the forms of service we can render, says Jesus, are relief to the poor, entertainment of the homeless, tending of the sick, comforting the sorrowful, and the reconciliation of those who are at feud (Matt. 5:9; 25:34-36). Then there are not only the social implications of the gospel so much to the fore today in all our relief programs for those in need at home and abroad, but the spiritual implications as well, namely, the salvation of souls from sin and efforts to help them rise to higher ends of excellence and nobility. Such double help for our neighbor must be disinterested service without any thought of return or reward (Matt. 6:2–4; Luke 6:34). The best service for our neighbor in any sphere loses its grace if we fail to help solely because we love our neighbor.

Discharging our duty toward neighbors, "each according to his ability," then, covers two realms. The seven corporal works of mercy described by Jesus are clothing the naked, giving drink to the thirsty, feeding the hungry, visiting the prisoners and the sick, relieving the poor, sheltering the homeless, and burying the dead. The seven spiritual works our neighbor requires are giving good counsel to those who need it, teaching the ignorant, discreetly correcting those who have offended, comforting those who are cast down, forgiving those who have injured us, patiently bearing reproach, and devoutly praying for those who are our neighbors.

In his teaching on neighborliness, Jesus lays quite an unexpected emphasis on sheer tenderness, on kindness to those in need and to strangers, the instinctive humanity that helps men, if it be only by the swift offer of a cup of cold water (Matt. 10:42). We emulate the example of Jesus, as the good Samaritan did, when we bear another's burden (Gal. 6:2). Illustrating his own tenderness toward those in need, Jesus used the impressive phrase of Isaiah, "A bruised reed shall he not break" (Isa. 42:3). He urged attention going beyond what is natural to man. "Do not even the publicans the same?" Loving our neighbor involves going a little further, even to taking the second mile (Matt. 5:41, 46). T. R. Glover comments that "the man who would use such compulsion would be an alien soldier, the hireling of Herod or of Rome; and who would wish to cart him and his goods even a mile?" "Go two miles," says Jesus, or, if the Syriac translation preserves the right reading, "Go two *extra*." Ordinary kindness and tenderness could hardly be urged beyond the first mile; yet Jesus goes further still. With an instinctive love and friendliness he could even pray for those of his neighbors who despitefully used him (Matt. 5:44; Luke 23:34).

An Anglican prayer for The Twenty-third Sunday after Trinity reads:

> Grant me to love my neighbor as myself, and to do to all men as I would they should do unto me,— to hurt nobody by word or deed, and to do my Duty in that state of life unto which it shall please Thee to call me!

Said Marcus Aurelius, Roman emperor of the second century:

> Every man has three relations to acquite himself in:
> His body that encompasses him makes one;
> The Divine Cause that gives to all men all things, another;
> His neighbour a third.

The poet T. Lyte would have us pray, "Teach me what I owe to Man below / And to Thyself in Heaven!"

—4—

False Love

That *love,* the ardent emotion of the heart, can be centered on wrong objects of affection, as well as on good and beneficial objects, also emerges from what the Master taught about such a theme. In this particular, the scribes and Pharisees were the worst sinners, and Jesus spared no words in unmasking their false objects of love. He called them hypocrites because "They *love* to pray standing in the synagogues and in the corners of the streets, that they may be seen of men" (Matt. 6:5). These loveless religious leaders knew nothing of the love and joy of praying to God in secret. Truly, these men had their *reward,* by which Jesus meant they got at once *all they will ever get,* namely, the admiration of those who witnessed their show-off.

They "*love* the uppermost rooms at feasts" (Matt. 23:6). By *uppermost,* we understand the "best" rooms that could be had. Because of their hypocritical religious practices they passed over, or neglected, "the judgement and the love of God" (Luke 11:42). They also "Loved greetings in the markets" (Luke 20:46). And because they craved after the honor of men, the love of God was not in them, said Jesus (John 5:42). Evidently there were those among the Pharisees who came to believe that Jesus was the Messiah that Isaiah had predicted, but they were afraid to confess him, lest they should be excluded from the synagogue in which they had play-acted because "They *loved* the praise of men more than the praise of God" (John 12:43). Godet translates the phrase, "They loved the glory which comes from men more than the glory which comes from God." If only they had loved to live only for God's glory, what enjoyment of his benediction would have been theirs!

Paul is not the only apostle to give us a notable "Hymn of Love," as 1 Corinthians 13 has been called. John, his fellow apostle, likewise has a virtual hymn to the divine love in his first Epistle. We find him warning the saints against the wrong kind of love: "Love not the world, neither the things in the world. If any man love the world, the love of the Father is not in him" (1 John 2:15).

It goes without saying that there are so many wonderful things in God's created world for us to love. The *world,* however, which John urges the children of God not to set their heart upon, is the present world system or the sum total of human life in an ordered world hostile to God, organized by Satan, the god of this world of lost sinners, into "the world of unbelieving mankind upon his cosmic principles of force, greed, selfishness, ambition, and pleasure" (Matt. 4:5, 9; John 12:31; Eph. 2:2; 6:12; 1 John 2:11–17). John, himself, describes the world he had in mind as being made up of "The lust of the flesh, the lust of the eyes, the pride of life" (1 John 2:16).

Such a world is a false object of our heart's love, seeing it is not only detrimental to life now, but is, with its lust, to pass away. It is a world of unsaved humanity inspired by its satanic prince, the atmosphere of which is immoral and which "at every moment of our lives we inhale, again inevitably exhale." The strange thing is that the word John uses for *love* in connection with a lustful, lost world, is *agapaō*, the same word he used of God's love for a lost race of sinners, the love which he is by nature, and the love which is produced in the heart of the yielded saint by the Holy Spirit (John 3:16; 1 John 4:8; Gal. 5:22).

Further, this Greek term *agapaō* is used in the classical meaning of love called out of one's heart by the preciousness of the object loved and thus refers to a fondness, an affection, nonethical in content, for an object because of its value. It is a love of approbation, of esteem. Paul sorrowfully wrote that "Demas loved this present world." This deserter of the apostle found the world of pleasure precious and thus came to love it. The phrase, "love not," carried the idea of "an act of forbidding the continuance of an action already going on." Some to whom John wrote were loving the things of the world, from which they had been saved, and so warned, "Stop loving the world with a love called out of your hearts because of its fancied preciousness."

Emphatically John declares that one who is guilty of the continuous, habitual action of loving the world with its lust is destitute of the love of the Father. Such precious love *is not in him.* Vincent, in his *Word Studies,* comments that "this means more than he does not love God: rather, that the love of God does not dwell in him as the ruling principle of his life." Actually, he is an unsaved person. Westcott, the renowned commentator, cites a parallel from Philo: "It is impossible for love to the world to co-exist with love to God, as it is impossible for light and darkness to coexist."

If "Abba, Father!" is the cry of newborn filial love (Rom. 8:15; Gal. 4:6), then its antithesis is found in false and futile objects of love, such as "the world," "self," "pleasure," and "money" (Luke 16:13; John 15:19–24; 2 Tim 3:2–5; James 4:4).

Thy name is Love! I hear it from yon Cross;
  Thy name is Love! I read it in yon tomb;
All meaner love is perishable dross,
  But this shall light me through time's thickest gloom.

What a fitting end to our topic of *Love* is the exclamation of Thomas à Kempis: "Oh how powerful is the pure love of Jesus, which is mixed with no self-interest, nor self-love!"

BIBLE STUDY QUESTIONS

Take time to turn to each Scripture reference and mark the verse or a portion in your Bible.

1. What is the meaning of love as used in the Bible?
2. Whom did God love and who should love him?
3. How did Christ show his love and what does he expect of us?
4. To whom should human love be directed?
5. What love did Jesus warn against?

— 5 —

About Marriage and Divorce

As we are endeavoring in these studies to examine the topics the Master taught, as they are recorded in the Gospels, our findings will reveal how opposed they are to the estimation of our modern, permissive society in the matters of marriage and divorce. Family life would have been on a much higher level today if only it had been fashioned according to the teaching of Jesus regarding marriage and home vows and value. How he denounced the deadly foe ruining homes, and through them, the nation! History proves that the multiplication of broken homes through divorce and the decay of nations and of social systems have gone hand in hand. In his *Decline and Fall of the Roman Empire,* Edward Gibbon wrote of the prevalence of divorce as a prominent cause of Rome's decline:

> When the Roman matrons became the equal and voluntary companions of their lords, a new jurisprudence was established, that marriage, like other partnerships, might be dissolved by the abdication of one of the associates. In three centuries of prosperity and corruption, this principle was enlarged to frequent practice and pernicious abuses. Passion, interest, or caprice suggested daily motives for the dissolution of

> marriage: a word, a sign, a message, a letter, the mandate of a freeman, declared the separation: the most tender of human connections was degraded to a transient society of profit and of pleasure.

Laws, the renowned missionary, who had an unsurpassed knowledge of savage peoples, once remarked that the place of any race on the upward or downward scale could be accurately measured by their relation to two of the Ten Commandments—the fifth and the seventh—"Thou shalt not commit adultery" and "Thou shalt not bear false witness against thy neighbour." Dr. Laws could have added, "Thou shalt not covet . . . thy neighbour's wife."

A graver situation has arisen in this twentieth century when marriage is outmoded, and people, principally those in the world of entertainment, live together without any solemn contract, have children, separate, then settle down to live in sin with others. Where marriage is entered into, whether in a religious or civil ceremony, it can be easily dissolved. In fact, a pair can divorce and remarry as often as they like. On the slightest pretext now, a marriage can be broken up, as the soaring rate of divorces proves. Perhaps we should now change the marriage line, "For better or for worse . . . till death doth us part," to "till divorce does us part."

It would seem as if divorce is competing with death as a dissolver of marriages. At the present rate of increase there will soon be more marriages dissolved by the courts than those consummated by pastors and priests and magistrates. The purpose, as well as the perpetuity of marriage, then, make it imperative for us to know what Jesus taught on such a prominent subject and to realize that what he taught has never been abrogated and, therefore, is applicable today. Loose views on marriage and divorce, although they may be hailed as signs of emancipation of society from the fetters of ignorance, superstition, and prejudice, result in a low standard of morality and a weakening of the moral strength of a nation. A true, wholesome family life has a far-reaching influence upon the formation of Christian character of those in the home, and any God-fearing nation owes power and influence to the recognition of Christ in its homes.

Believing that Christ has the answer to any personal or public problem, our task is to state what he taught and commanded. We are not to concern ourselves with the many opinions about marriage and divorce, or even with what the church, Protestant or Roman, may teach and command about such a subject. Our sole criterion is, *What did Jesus teach?* On a few social questions he was noncommittal, but the social matter on which he spoke full and explicitly was the nature and duration of marriage. His high conception is seen in his use of the marriage relationship to illustrate union with himself. Paul could write of being "married to the Lord." The relationship in the home—that of parents with the children—was a picture of the bond between God and his own (Matt. 7:7–11).

THE MARRIAGE OF ONE MAN AND ONE WOMAN IS A DIVINE INSTITUTION

Quoting from the creation record (Gen. 2:23–25), Jesus declared marriage to be of divine origin and as a fundamental social order to be recognized as such. When tempted by the Pharisees to give his opinion as to the divorce of married people, he said, "Have ye not read, that he which made them at the beginning made them male and female, and said, For this cause shall a man leave father and mother, and shall cleave to his wife: and they twain shall be one flesh? Wherefore they are no more twain, but one flesh. What therefore God hath joined together, let not man put asunder" (Matt. 19:4–6).

Such a clear, positive statement was the reply of Jesus to the cunning purpose of the Pharisees to trap Jesus on the legality of divorce. Clarence Macartney says that their subtle purpose was twofold, *first,* to get from Jesus an utterance which might be construed as a condemnation of the ruler of their country, Herod Antipas—who was living with his brother Philip's wife—and so stir up his anger against Jesus; *second,* to draw from Jesus a saying which would seem to be in disagreement with Moses and the Old Testament. But he took his questioners back to Moses and enforcing his teaching declared that *monogamy*—one man living with one woman as prescribed by the Creator —was the divine and original plan for marriage.

The Pharisees went back to the Law, citing the divorce legislation of Moses as the authorization of divorce, but Jesus took them back to the original plan of God and summoned them back to the divine institution of marriage in which man and woman formed a union which was indisoluble once it had been contracted. To break such a union, by violating it and marrying another, was to commit adultery. The human race by the will, purpose, and power of God began with a monogamous union between man and woman—a mutual union, natural and inevitable, which only death could break. Jesus, then, went right back to God's intent, not to man's treatment of marriage, but to God's thought and meaning of the institution. God ordained marriage. He was the one who planned it, and such a union of man and woman takes on a solemn significance when it is thought of in this way. His specific precepts and strong words in regard to divorce must be connected with an experience of the home that was happy in itself and that he regarded as according to the divine plan (Matt. 5:27–32).

Although Jesus himself did not marry and did not teach, as the rabbis did, that marriage was obligatory for all (Matt. 19:12), he considered such a union to be a divinely established one and required absolute purity in it, affirming that even looking at another man's wife "to lust after her" was adultery. Jesus also taught that marriage belongs to this created world in which we live but that in the world to come it will have no validity (Matt. 22:30). Shakespeare's lines on the blessedness and sweetness of the mutual yoke of man and wife as ordained of God are apt at this point:

> He is the half part of a blessed man,
> Left to be finished by such as she;
> And she a fair divided excellence,
> Whose fulness of perfection lies in him.

The first to pervert the divine order of marriage was Lamech, the descendant of Cain, who initiated polygamy (Gen. 4:16–24). *Monogamy* means marriage with but one person at a time, or the only marriage during life. *Polygamy,* however, is the state or fact of having a plurality of wives, at the same time. Lamech was the first bigamist and, if alive and in our country today, would be jailed for marrying a second woman while still lawfully married to his first wife. After Lamech, polygamy became more widespread with even leaders of Israel, like Jacob, Saul, David, and Solomon having more than one wife. Like other sins, this one was endured by God but never approved, seeing it was in direct opposition to his original intent of the marriage bond. Mankind began with a monogamous and for life, still stands. A married woman through sin man fell in polygamy, divorce, and kindred corruptions of the divine order.

The apostolic enforcement and extension of the teaching of Jesus as to marriage being monogamous and for life, still stands. "A married woman is bound by law to her husband [and vice versa] as long as he lives; but if her husband dies she is discharged from the law concerning her husband. Accordingly, she will be called an adulteress if she lives with another man while her husband is alive. But if her husband dies she is free from that law and if she marries another man she is not an adulteress" (Rom. 7:2–3, RSV; see 1 Cor. 7:39, 40).

How sweet the mutual yoke of Man and Wife,
When holy fires maintain Love's heavenly life!

THE MARRIAGE OF ONE MAN AND ONE WOMAN IS A DIVINE ACT

Without doubt, the first marriage on earth was made by heaven, but heaven has no part in the six marriages of an actor or actress with all previous wives or husbands still living. What a mockery of such a divine institution this is! Jesus said, "They are no more twain, but one flesh. What therefore God hath joined together, let not man put asunder" (Matt. 19:6; Gen. 2:23–25; 4:1, 2). Both Adam and Jesus emphasize the fact that in creating man, God made one woman for one man, and that monogamy is to be the rule of man; and any rules which covertly or openly permit to man a plurality of wives, stand condemned by the precedent of the Garden of Eden. Adam registered the truth that in marriage man and wife become one flesh; and, being so joined, may not be put asunder.

While our courts rip asunder an ever-increasing number of marriages and allow those parted to remarry others almost immediately, the universal reason of man feels that the grounds of indissoluble union are valid and conclusive and that the proper view of marriage treats it as a union, binding "as long as both shall live." A home happy in itself was regarded by Jesus as being according to the divine plan. While the patriarchs and others in Old Testament times had many wives, and the Mosaic law allowed a man to put away his wife (Deut. 24:1), Jesus taught that his followers must rise above such a level and accept his teaching that the marriage bond must not be severed and that both the man and the woman are equally bound by it (Mark 10:10–12; see 1 Cor. 7:10, 11; Gal. 3:28). For this reason the sacredness and permanence of the marriage relation is likened to the relationship of the Christian to Christ (Eph. 5:28–30).

The happiest marriages are those in which husband and wife believe they were joined together, as such, by the Lord and fully and equally share each other's lives, continually lifting them up to God. Marriages of this sort, in which cares, trials, and responsibilities are met by united prayer and thought and single purpose, are indeed made in heaven and continually blessed by heaven. When two are joined together by the Lord in his sanctuary, then the function of the church is threefold: to bear witness to their lifelong vows when they consent together in holy wedlock; to pronounce God's blessing upon the pair when they enter, of their own accord, into this holy estate; to guard the sanctity of the marriage bond as long as they both shall live.

How appealing are the lines of Lewis Morris on wedded life.

> The world hath need of all of you—
> Hath need of you, and of thee, too, fair Love.
> Oh Lovers, cling together! The old world
> Is full of Hate. Sweeten it! draw in one
> Two separate chords of Life; and from the bond
> Of twin souls lost in Harmony, create
> A Fair God dwelling with you—Love, the Lord!

THE MARRIAGE OF ONE MAN AND ONE WOMAN UNIFIES HUSBAND AND WIFE SO THAT THEY CEASE TO BE TWO AND BECOME ONE FLESH

Twice over Jesus used the phrase, "*They* twain shall be *one* flesh" (Matt. 19:5–6). *One flesh.* The term *cleave* he employed denotes a union of the closest and firmest kind. The original word is taken from *gluing* and means so firmly to *adhere* together that nothing can separate or unglue them. Husband and wife were *two* but became united as *one* in law, in feeling, in interest, and in affection. No longer are there separate and personal interests, but both act in all things as if they were one, animated by one soul and one wish.

In his reply to the cunning question of the Pharisees as to marriage and divorce, Jesus declared that since two are so intimately joined as to be one, and since in the beginning God made but one woman for one man, it follows that they cannot be separated but by the authority of God. Man may *not* put away his wife for every cause. What *God* hath joined together, *man* may not put asunder. To divide *one flesh,* or to unmarry two who have been united, is to destroy a living organism. The word *asunder* Jesus used is most suggestive. We read that some early Christians were "sawn asunder" (Heb. 11:37), and this is the kind of murder so prevalent today. The courts of our land, quite easily and quickly, saw asunder those who in God's sight are organically one, and they are thus murdering the home life of our land. "What God doeth, it shall be for ever" (Eccles. 3:14).

Further, the annulment of the marriage bond is foreign to the teaching of Jesus in which he says that marriage binds one man and one woman together in a relationship closer and more binding than that between parent and child. "For this cause shall a man leave father and mother, and shall cleave to his wife" (Matt. 19:5). This quotation which Jesus used with approval from Genesis 2:24 means but one thing, namely, that when a man takes a wife he binds himself more strongly to his partner than he was to his father or mother. In the mind of Jesus the marriage bond is the most tender and endearing of all human relations, more tender even than the bond which unites us to a parent. In his chapter on "The Family" in *The Ethic of Jesus,* Professor James Stalker, dealing with the mysterious attraction drawing opposite sexes into marriage, says:

> No wonder the Saviour alluded to this strong attraction of a pair drawn away from their own home to found a new one with such high appreciation; for, if the aim of Christianity is to purge the heart of selfishness, it can find in the world nothing so akin to itself as pure love between the sexes, which carries the person possessed with it completely out of himself and makes all sacrifices for the sake of the beloved object easy. In some, no doubt, this is transient, the mere blazing up of a flame which is soon extinguished. But in the multitude of cases it is enduring. The choice is a permanent one, and the union only becomes more close and sacred the longer it lasts. If to first love, as it is called, there attached a beauty which has evoked the enthusiasm of poets and romancers, the love of old age is not less beautiful, when it has survived all the changes and chances of life, only becoming mellower with the passage of years.

An anonymous poet of a past century, dealing with the consecration of wedded life lived as God meant, has left us the stanza:

> We in our wedded life shall know no loss,
> We shall new-date our years! What went before
> Will be the time of promise, shadow, dream:
> But this, full revelation of great love;
> For rivers blent take in a broader heaven,
> And we shall bend our souls!

THE MARRIAGE OF ONE MAN AND ONE WOMAN IS A RELATIONSHIP WHICH DEATH, AND NOT DIVORCE, CAN DISSOLVE

In the plan of God, and in the teaching of Jesus, the marriage pact is for life; when man and woman are joined together, they should become heirs together of the grace of life, while life lasts, with death alone being the dissolver of the union. A proverb among the Veddahs of Ceylon reads, "Death alone separates husband and wife." In our human society the enduring length of marriage is a real guide to the strength of love and of its quality. In this remaining section we concern ourselves, primarily, with the question of divorce as dealt with by Jesus. With the alarming increase of broken marriages by this cruel dissolver of the sacred bond, it is most necessary to know what the Master taught in order to combat the growing evil of easy ways out of what is called the Sacrament of Marriage.

When Jesus spoke on any theme, in every case he stated the absolute and uncompromising demand of God. "I have given them thy word" (John 17:14). To the honest reader it is perfectly clear that the New Testament, as a whole, is utterly opposed to divorce and that, in particular, the word of Jesus on the subject is absolute and should be literally obeyed, no matter how such an insistence is contrary to modern practices of dissolving the contract of two who were made one in holy matrimony for better or for worse. It should be the solemn obligation of all who officiate at marriages to state clearly what Jesus taught as the divine intent and permanency of the sacred union

—a union that must not be severed and one by which the man and the woman are equally bound. The only references to divorce in the Gospels are all associated with the one encounter between the Pharisees and Jesus on the subject. Differences can be noted if we set these references alongside each other.

Matthew 5:31	*Matthew 5:32*
"It hath been said, Whosoever shall put away his wife, let him give her a writing of divorcement:"	"But I say unto you, That whosoever shall put away his wife, saving for the cause of fornication, causeth her to commit adultery: and whosoever shall marry her that is divorced committeth adultery."
Mark 10:5, 6	*Mark 10:11–12*
"Jesus answered and said unto them, For the hardness of your heart he wrote you this precept. But from the beginning of the creation God made them male and female. . . ."	"Whosoever shall put away his wife, and marry another, committeth adultery against her. And if a woman shall put away her husband, and be married to another, she committeth adultery."
1 Corinthians 7:10–11	*Luke 16:18*
"Let not the wife depart from her husband: But and if she depart,	"Whosoever putteth away his wife, and marrieth another, commit-

let her remain unmarried, or be reconciled to her husband: and let not the husband put away his wife."

teth adultery: and whosoever marrieth her that is put away from her husband committeth adultery."

Matthew 19:9

"Whosoever shall put away his wife, except it be for fornication, and shall marry another, committeth adultery: and whoso marrieth her which is put away doth commit adultery."

Note: Deuteronomy 24:1–4 should be studied along with these passages from the Gospels.

A consideration of these parallel passages leads one to a few observations, important in nature. First, Jesus uses two words, namely, *fornication* and *adultery*, which certainly do not mean the same thing. *Fornication* means uncleanness between those who are unmarried; *adultery* implies uncleanness between persons one of whom, at least, is married.

Moses never gave a writing of divorcement in the case of adultery, for the penalty of adultery was death, and there was no exception. "The adulterer shall surely be put to death" (Lev. 20:10). Jesus at least implied that this was a righteous law when he said, "He that is without sin among you, let him first cast a stone" (John 8:7).

Under the law of Moses the husband was permitted to put away his wife if she found no favor in his eyes because he had found some uncleanness in her, which evidently referred to sin committed *before* marriage (Deut. 24:1). Discovering that he had married an unvirtuous woman, he could put her away, but the words of Jesus give no permission to remarry, for the phrase, "her that is divorced," is only one word in the Greek and means "a divorced woman."

Actually, then, Jesus said that "whosoever shall put away his wife and marry a divorced woman committeth adultery." Thus, in the light of the law of Moses it is clear that Jesus used the word *fornication* in its usual sense of uncleanness before marriage and distinguishes it from adultery (Matt. 15:19; Mark 7:21; see Gal. 5:19). "The writing of divorcement" was only given to the man who discovered after marriage the unchaste character of his wife, but even this Jesus declared was due to the hardness of the hearts of those concerned and not to any commandment of God. Hence, the emphatic statement, "From the beginning it was not so" (Matt. 19:8). In such a statement Jesus appeals from the temporary concession of Moses to the eternal, original law of God, namely, that he made male and female, one man and one woman, with no provision of separation or divorce.

We all know that that first marriage did not turn out very well, divinely planned though it was, for the husband was enticed by the wife into sin, and both husband and wife learned to know what a broken heart means when they stood over the corpse of their son, Abel, slain by the hand of his brother Cain, earth's first murderer (Gen. 4:1–8). But Adam and Eve remained together and doubtless found family happiness when other sons and daughters were born to them (Gen. 5:4). It was

Lamech who began the departure from the monogamic bond by introducing polygamy which opened the gate of promiscuity. When Israel became a nation, a Hebrew could have two or more wives or concubines, also intercourse with a slave or bondwoman, even though married, without being reckoned guilty of the crime of adultery, because adultery, according to Jewish law, was possible only when a man dishonored the *free wife* of a Hebrew (Lev. 19:20 20:10).

In his teaching, however, Jesus was bold enough to be original in his affirmation that the Mosaic law of divorce had been an accommodation to the demand of men's hearts, while the only true annulment of marriage could be recognized and declared because of marital unfaithfulness. In fact, he went further and transferred the sin of adultery to the lustful desire, the act being fully condemned. The Pharisees were always on the alert to trap Jesus with a question, and his answers revealed the characteristics of his thinking. Instantly, he "recognizes their trickery" (Luke 20:23), and with a certain swiftness, the quick realization of a situation, a character, or the meaning of a word, had a ready reply. Thus when his persistent enemies, the Pharisees, asked Jesus, "Is it lawful for a man to put away his wife for *every cause,*" he had but one reply. He deliberately swept aside all other pretenses for divorce and named adultery per se destructive of monogamic family life.

An article by Dr. C. Caverno in the *International Standard Bible Encyclopedia* states:

> It is the hand of an unerring Master that has made fornication a ground of divorce from the bond of matrimony and limited divorce to that single cause.

> Whichever way we depart we depart from strict practice under the Saviour's direction, we land in polygamy—The society that allows by its statutes divorce for any other cause than the one that breaks the monogamic bond, is simply acting in aid of polygamy, consecutive if not contemporaneous.

Today, there are numerous easy roads out of marriage such as desertion, cruelty, lack of support, drunkenness, incompatibility, and others somewhat ludicrous in character. By affording easy ways out of the trials of married life we invite carelessness about entering marriage. By just as much as a crevice for relief of the miseries of married life is opened by divorce, by so much the flood gates are opened into these miseries. The more solemnly society is impressed that the door of marriage does not swing outward as well as inward the more of happiness and blessing will it find in the institution.

There has developed an idea, particularly in some Protestant churches, that the traditional ban against the remarriage of divorced persons should be considerably softened, and so there is the agreement to remarry *the innocent party* to a divorce. But in the break-up of a home it is to be questioned whether there is any *innocent party.* Usually, the dissolution is caused by mutual, contributing factors. But over against all supposed grounds for divorce is the absolute word of Jesus—"Saving for the cause of adultery." Both Jesus and Paul exalted marriage to heights of significance and sanctity unknown under the old covenant, for in their teaching they sought to restore matrimony to its state and honor as intended by God at creation (Mark 10:9; see Heb. 13:4; 1 Cor. 7:10–16). The phrase "the husband of one wife" (1 Tim. 3:2, 12;

Titus 1:6) is given in the Revised Version as "married only once," the meaning of which is obvious.

Some theologians have suggested that the teaching of Jesus on divorce as given in Matthew 5 is contrary to his words on the subject in Mark 10 and in Luke 16. In Matthew's account divorce is permitted on the grounds of infidelity; in Mark and Luke divorce seems to be forbidden on any ground whatever. The most satisfactory explanation of this seeming contradiction is that what is stated *explicitly* by Jesus in Matthew is *implicit* in Mark and Luke; that the exception stated in Matthew—"Saving for the cause of adultery"—is assumed by Mark and Luke who take for granted Matthew's account of the conversation of Jesus on the divorce question. That Paul is in agreement with Jesus, whose *mind* the apostle said he had, is evident from the command, "The woman which hath a husband is bound by the law to her husband so long as he liveth. . . . So then if, while her husband liveth, she is married to another man, she shall be called an adulteress" (Rom. 7:2–3).

In many parts of the world today divorce is the open sore of mankind, and it is incumbent upon pastors, in particular, to stress that the strictness of the marriage bond as taught by Jesus is the security of morals and of family welfare. All should unite in opposing movements and arguments for permitting divorce for any reason short of the act Jesus mentioned which ruptures the bond between man and wife. Undivided homes are the supreme social necessity for national well-being, religious prosperity, and individual advantage. Whatever those of loose morals may have to say of the increasing sexual permissiveness of today, the fact cannot be disputed that such behavior is totally prohibited by the teaching of Jesus and his apostles. Richard Glover in his most valuable commentary on *Matthew* summarizes the subject:

1. Facilities of divorce, except on the ground of adultery, are proofs of a low state of self-respect in any community, and tend to lower it still more.
2. They work incalculable mischief, for such facilities prevent the healing of quarrels, and unions which might have become sources of honourable comfort, and often promote the sins which are the grounds of separation.
3. Stringency of marriage laws in the interest of the women and the children everywhere. Their rights should be protected.
4. The true secrets for preventing matrimonial misery are:

   Greater care in entering marriage engagements—
   Full mutual knowledge before engagements to marry are made—
   Unselfishness—
   Action in the fear of the Lord—
   The repression of all Lust—
   Above all things—LOVE.
5. The surest way to a happy marriage is:

   To deserve a good husband or wife—
   Only to marry one it is a pleasure to serve—
   To marry only in the Lord, and to bear with all patience and meekness anything not according to expectations—
   If unhappily mated, loving endurance is still both wisdom and duty—
   To keep an unbroken home for children:
   To save them from dishonour and hurt—
   To practice patience—these are things which have great reward.

When Jesus, in reply to the question asked by the Pharisees, "Why did Moses command to give a writing of divorcement?" said, "Because of the hardness of your hearts, suffered you to put away your wives," he implied that Moses acted on the divine principle of suffering evil to exist, but which is divinely disapproved. As Christians, we are not to govern our conduct by the evils which God suffers *but by the law which he gives,* and in his teaching, Jesus gave us the law of God for *all* ages which stated simply is: There may be *divorce* for adultery, and it may be wise to *separate* for other causes, but remarriage *never,* and thus the way is open to repentance and reunion. Pleading with adulterous Israel to turn from her sin, God's plea was, "For I am married unto you" (Jer. 3:14), and he promised to receive her back if only she would repent (Jer. 2, 3). If sin has broken up a home, it is possible for repentance and regeneration to restore it, but such a possibility is forever precluded by remarriage on the heels of divorce.

Both the sacredness and indissolubility of the marriage bond is found in the use of it as a beautiful metaphor of the relationship between Christ and his church. After leaving the home in which he lived for thirty years in an atmosphere conducive to his spiritual development and happiness, his first public appearance was at a wedding. His mother was present, and he contributed to the happiness of the occasion by performing his first miracle of turning water into the best wine. In his parable on the wise and foolish virgins, Jesus used the figure of the marriage to enforce the truth of his Second Advent (Matt. 25:1–13), and John describes for us the marriage of the Lamb (Rev. 19:7–9).

Paul's lofty conception of the bond between Christ and his church is incomparable: "Wives, submit yourselves unto your own husbands, as unto the Lord. For the husband is the head of the wife, even as Christ is the head of the church: and he is the saviour of the body. Therefore as the church is subject unto Christ, so let the wives be to their own husbands in every thing. Husbands, love your wives, even as Christ also loved the church, and gave himself for it" (Eph. 5:22–25). If the relationship between husband and wife can be a figure of the union of the eternal and majestic Christ with his bride, the church, then how high and beautiful ought to be the marriage union between the man and the woman. Paul also uses the divine teaching on the indissolubility of the marriage bond to illustrate his eternal relationship to Jesus Christ his Lord (Rom. 7:1–6).

From Him, Who loves me now so well,
  What power my soul can sever?
Shall life, or death, or earth, or Hell?
  No: I am His for ever.

BIBLE STUDY QUESTIONS

Take time to turn to each Scripture reference and mark the verse or a portion in your Bible.

1. Why is the marriage relationship so important in the New Testament?

2. How did Jesus regard marriage and divorce?

3. What is the explanation of "they twain shall be one flesh"?

4. What actions are Biblical in the matters of fornication and adultery?

5. As Christians what should govern our conduct, and why?

— 6 —

About Women

For a rewarding insight into our Lord's attitude toward, and teaching about, *women* while he tabernacled here below, it is essential to understand the Roman and the Jewish estimation of woman during the first century. Born into a world under Roman domination and named a *Jew* by a woman of questionable character, Jesus became familiar with the treatment accorded women by religious and heathen rulers alike. And it is such treatment that lends color to his contact with women and to his conversation with and about them.

Under Roman law, operating at the time when Jesus was born of a woman, women were under the perpetual tutelage of their male relatives. C. Loring Brace, in his erudite work *Gesta Christi* (What Christ Hath Wrought), gives us an insight into the restricted life of women under the old Roman laws. They could not intervene in the government of the family, nor in industrial or commercial affairs, nor in public matters. A court of the relatives of a woman could inflict upon her the severest penalties in case of certain offenses. She was not the equal of her husband but treated, more or less, as an adopted ward. All her property became her husband's; all her earnings were his; her children need not obtain her consent to marry, for the children were not reckoned to be in the family of the mother but of the father. She was not a person in her own right. But under Justinian laws, absolute power of the husband over his wife and her property ceased.

With the coming of Jesus and his gospel, there developed a new conception of the worth and position of women, and the tendency toward "the personal and proprietary independence" of women in modern law and custom received its first great stimulus in the religion of Jesus affecting Roman law. Through Christianity, the elevated position of women and the character of the relation between husband and wife, with emphasis on the absolute sacredness of such a union, became apparent. The new faith threw a halo about woman she has never lost. As Loring Brace convincingly proves, such female emancipation came about as the results of the character and teachings of Jesus.

> The power of Christianity on the Roman world was especially the influence of a Person, of a pure and elevated character who claimed to be a supernatural Being in His relations with men and God, and Who was the Founder of a new religion. His nature alone, from its purity and elevation, seemed to sweep away unnatural pas-

sions from among men, both in the Roman Empire, and since among all races following Him.

Through the influence of the great Friend of women, their changed position resulted in continual reproach by the early enemies of the Christians because they gave their women high position in the church. And as we know from the Acts and the Epistles, women came to exercise a strong influence in the church. Further, as the result of Christ's teaching, the original conception of marriage as a bond of equal union, and the highest spiritual partnership, was restored. Paul taught that in marriage two became one flesh. Alas! however, in non-Christian lands, the misery of women can be seen whether in marriage among Mohammedans or widowhood in Hinduism.

In Jewish circles, also, the teaching of Jesus concerning women and his treatment of them caused the Pharisees, whose approach to women was so different from his own, to rise up in protest against his respectful and sympathetic understanding of their needs and trials. An old Jewish prayer read, "Blessed art thou, O Lord our God! King of the Universe, Who hast not made me a woman." How wonderfully did Jesus, firstborn of Mary, change the world of women! We never find him warning men against women. As T. R. Glover reminds us in *The Jesus of History:*

> Even the most degraded woman finds in him an amazing sympathy; for he has the secret of being pure and kind at the same time—his purity has not to be protected; it is itself a purifying

force. Jesus draws some of his most delightful Parables from woman's work. It is recorded how, when he spoke of the coming disasters of Jerusalem, he paused to pity poor pregnant women and mothers with little babies in those bad times. Matt. 24:19; Luke 21:23.

Bishop Gore, in dealing with various aspects of Jesus' teaching, does not fail to notice his attitude toward women. He comments in *Jesus of Nazareth:*

> There was a good deal in the sacred literature of Israel tending to give a high status to women, but on the whole it would be true to say that they were still treated as the chattels and instruments of men. Contemptuous references to womankind can easily be quoted from the Old Testament and the Rabbis: Jesus showed no disposition to include women among his apostles or official agents: but he constantly treated women as of the same spiritual worth as men. He is represented as talking freely to them in public places contrary to the Jewish custom. When he had to do with "fallen women" he totally refused to treat them with contempt or under a "taboo." He welcomed their repentance and set them free. In his ministry of mercy he showed the same regard to women as men. For a part of his ministry at least a company of women was attached to the company of the disciples and ministered to them of their substance. Women, like Martha and Mary, were among his friends and he thought them worthy of his highest teaching. He saw in them, that is, the same spiritual worth and capacity as men.

The attitude of Jesus is of primary importance, for it has been largely influential in the vast change in women's place in the home and in society. To him they owe the rights of persons to be personalities. As we study the

Gospels, we find how all women, good and bad, were attracted to Jesus because, in the true sense of the word, he was a *gentleman.* With all confidence, mothers brought their children to him to be blessed. Sisters, like Mary and Martha, loved to have Jesus in their home, and, as one writer puts it, "It would not be at all surprising if they loved him as a woman loves a true man." Good women, enriched by his teaching, gladly ministered unto him of their substance.

As for his own holy estimation of women, is it not proven, in that before he left heaven, he chose Mary to be his mother, and after his victory over death elected another Mary to be the first herald of his resurrection? Jesus, then, in his attitude to women, referred men's thoughts back to the standard of God's thoughts concerning man's helpmate and supported what he taught by what he *was.* He regarded both man and woman as subject to the same divine laws, which were equally high for both sexes. Always he thought of the woman at least as much as of the man. It is in his human contacts that we discover his chief contribution to the higher view and the better treatment of womanhood. Each contact is a revelation of the mind of Jesus in relation to women who often wept for him.

JESUS AND HIS MOTHER

Although our knowledge of the family life of Jesus for thirty years is somewhat meager, we can safely assume that his attitude toward women generally was an outgrowth of a deep and happy relationship with his mother and sisters, of whom there must have been at least two. Did not his strong words in regard to *divorce* suggest the personal experience of a home that was happy in itself and fashioned according to the divine plan of family life? Can there be any doubt that mother love was a very important factor in the teaching of Jesus, as well as in his life? Do we not have echoes of the home at Nazareth in which he grew to manhood in his keen sense and instruction of the value of the child (Mark 10:13–16; Matt. 18:1–6)? Then what about his strong conviction as to duty to parents when he expressed his deep indignation of the Pharisees who taught negligence of parents as part of their service to God (Matt. 15:1–9)? Does not such explicit teaching imply that from his home life and from his actual relationship to his own parents there emerged his clear ideas of the relation of parents to children and vice versa?

Go back to the joyful song of Mary over the birth of her firstborn and of all the rich promise that such a lowly birth held (Luke 1:46–55). It is not hard to imagine Mary's growing delight and wonder as "the Holy Child Jesus" grew in stature and in favor with God and man; her constant questioning as to what the future held as she pondered in her heart one thing and another; her temporary misunderstanding and desire to drag him back to the sheltered and delightful home life. Mary knew from angelic and human announcements at the birth of her illustrious Son that he was born to die as the Savior of the world and the deepening appreciation that his great mission could only be fulfilled through pain—a pain which drove a sword into his mother's heart.

Although it may appear as if he treated his mother aloofly when he had to rebuke her gently for giving a personal relationship precedence over the spiritual bond, he was ever considerate of her and revered her as "blessed above women." Had she not his deepest thought in the agony of death? In the hour of extreme anguish his thought turned to the future welfare of the mother who had borne him, and he made provision for her in the home of John, the disciple whom Jesus loved. With the weight of the world's sin upon him, and the endurance of physical and spiritual agony beyond our imagining, Jesus addressed two sentences to his beloved mother and dearest friend, revealing, thereby, the tender relations which had existed between mother and Son: To Mary his mother, "Behold thy Son!" To John the disciple, "Behold thy mother" (John 19:26, 27).

A striking evidence of the deep affection of Mary for her Son, and of her determination to remain near him, encouraging him by her presence until the last moment of his intense physical suffering, is seen in her attitude at Calvary. Other women who loved Jesus stood *afar off,* beholding him die. Some of the disciples had forsaken him and fled. But what of Mary? We read that *she stood by the cross* (John 19:25, 26). She was not prostrate on the ground with grief as we might have expected a mother to be as she watched her firstborn die such a terrible death. We further read that her dying Son saw his mother *standing*, along with his beloved disciple, John, and, impressed by her brave watch, provided her with a new home.

The ministry of Jesus, then, grew out of his home life as the bud unfolds on the stem and colored his teaching as to a higher, larger, family life in which God is our heavenly Father and all redeemed by his blood are brothers and sisters. It is to be regretted that unhappy differences and divisions, acrimony and apostasy have greatly impaired the family love-mark that should ever characterize the church Jesus purchased by his precious blood (1 John 3).

JESUS AND WIDOWS

The Gospels record several contacts between Jesus and widows, and how kind, tender, and sympathetic he was in his treatment of them. Here, again, was it experience that made him so considerate of widowhood? After the episode in the Temple involving Jesus, Mary his mother, and Joseph his foster father, we have no further mention of Joseph, who vanishes altogether from the Gospel story. It is generally thought that he died some time after Jesus, at the age of fifteen, left the synagogue school and joined Joseph in the carpentery business. With his death, Jesus assumed control of the trade and became known as the "carpenter" and helped his widowed mother in every possible way to beat back the beast of poverty from the home in which its head was missing. With such a Son, how could Mary the widow be desolate?

It was a very aged widow who welcomed the birth of Jesus. Anna had long looked for the Redeemer to come in Jerusalem, and one day while at her usual prayers in the Temple, the glad tidings reached her of the Redeemer's appearance in the flesh, and she gave instant thanks (Luke 2:36–38).

When Jesus entered his public ministry, he had little sympathy with those religious leaders who took advantage of the helplessness of widows by devouring their houses (Matt. 23:14). The word for *houses* used here can denote property or possessions of any kind, which the scribes and Pharisees got possession of by improper pretenses. Barnes, in his *New Testament* commentary, explains:

> They pretended to a very exact knowledge of the Law, and to a perfect observance of it. They pretended to extraordinary justice to the poor, friendship for the distressed, and willingness to aid those who were in embarrassed circumstances. They thus induced *widows* and poor people to commit the management of their property to them as guardians and executors, and then took advantage of them, and defrauded them.

They then added to their heartless treatment of the poor widows by pretending to make long prayers for the women they were robbing. Those hypocrites felt they could the better defraud them by the appearance of sanctity, implying thereby that the widows were devoting their money to religious purposes and not lining the pockets of the callous Pharisees. Truly, the greater damnation is theirs.

With his intimate knowledge of the Old Testament, Jesus drew attention to widows in Israel in the time of Elijah, and particularly to the widow of Zarephath for whom the prophet miraculously provided food in days of famine (Luke 4:25, 26; 1 Kings 17:1–16). How bountifully was this widow's sacrifice rewarded!

The widow of Nain experienced the omnipotence of a greater prophet than Elijah (Luke 7:11–18). Among the many miracles of Jesus, the utterly unexpected one this sorrowing widow witnessed is one of the few cases where no appeal was made to Jesus to do anything. The action of Jesus was simply the overflow of his loving nature as he watched the only son of this grief-stricken woman being borne to the grave. Neighbors were all moved to pity for her, but there was nothing they could do but mingle their tears with those of the widow who had lost her only stay and support. The first word of Jesus to her was so like him, *Weep not!* The young man in his coffin almost seemed like a secondary consideration. The Divine Comforter's deed of mercy centered around the widow in her loneliness and grief. First, he wiped away her tears; then "he gave him back to his mother." The widow was of supreme importance to Jesus. Should not every bereaved mother find here something of peculiar solace?

Another widow who attracted the attention of Jesus was the one he watched casting all she had into the Temple treasury (Mark 12:38–44). There had been conflict with the Pharisees over their pretext of raising money for religious purposes when, actually, they had been draining away the resources of the very poor. Merciless to the widow and fatherless, these hypocrites, guilty of worthless generosity and empty prayers, gave nothing of their own to God. Jesus, turning from them with righteous indignation, caught sight of a widow quietly stealing up to the treasury and, as if ashamed of her very meager gift, slipping in the only two coins she possessed. Such an act was seen at its true worth by the eyes of him that ever pierces the sham and make-believe. Those *two mites,* representing a day's meat and drink—and *all* that she had—were an illustration of complete self-denial for God's sake. Jesus, who has his own standard of judgment, found in this godly widow a sacrifice winning his approval and commendation. The power to deny herself for God, the love that gives all and instinctively realizes that it will be accepted, is again a woman's.

In his parable of the unjust judge, Jesus describes a widow's importunate demand (Luke 18:1–8). Doubtless, he had met an actual widow of such persistence and here uses her to illustrate his parable that "men ought always to pray and not to faint." The judge, whose help she sought when pestered by an adversary, is described as *unjust,* "who feared not God, neither regarded man"—not a very commendable character for a judge. To get rid of this persistent widow, he offered judicial help, "lest by her continual coming she weary me." The word used here for *weary* denotes, in the original, the wounds and bruises caused by boxers who beat each other and disable themselves. In his application of the parable, Jesus revealed how different God is from the unjust judge. God values our perseverance and urges us not to faint in our oft coming to him, for suddenly and unexpectedly he will manifest justice on our behalf.

There can be no doubt, whatever, that the contacts of Jesus with widows and his kind and gracious treatment of them influenced the apostles to honor the widows who were widows indeed (1 Tim. 5:3–16; James 1:27). One reason for the election of deacons in the early church was for the caring of the widows who had been "neglected in the daily ministration" (Acts 6:1). Paul became conspicuous in his endeavor to continue and expand the Master's gracious treatment of those bereft of their partners in life. An Order of Widows developed in the church in the second century and lasted into the fourth, being abolished by the Council of Laodicaea in A.D. 364.

JESUS AND THE WOMAN WHO WAS A SINNER

Simon the Pharisee said "within himself," because he was afraid to say it audibly, "This man, if he were a prophet, would have known *who* and *what* manner of woman this is that toucheth him, for she is a sinner" (Luke 7:36–50). We gather from this that the woman of whom he spoke was an unchaste, disreputable person. No decent man should have any contact with her. Although a defiled creature, she knew Jesus was being entertained by Simon, and believing him to be a friend of sinners, she expressed her love and faith in him by washing his feet with her tears and drying them with the hairs of her head before anointing them with the very precious ointment she had brought. Twice during his life Jesus was anointed by a woman. Here, by one who had trodden dark and evil paths; in the other instance, by a pure saint, Mary of Bethany.

Was not this sinful woman who received the forgiving grace of Jesus—"Thy faith hath saved thee: go in peace"—more akin to the pure and sinless one than to the self-righteous Pharisee. Let it be noted that there is no record of any request from this woman, but hers was the quick instinct assuring her longing heart that here was one who would not spurn her, as men had done after satisfying their lust. She expressed her faith in the willingness of Jesus to deliver her from her sin by an act of pure love, and she was not disappointed. Jesus accepted the gift as an expression of her repentance and forgave her sins, which were many. She loved much and was fully forgiven. By contact with this sinful woman, Jesus was not defiled, as Simon thought he would be, for Simon's concept of a holy man was one who cannot touch evil. But a sunbeam loses nothing of its glory and purity by shining on a dunghill. Jesus, the thrice holy one, ever glories in lifting up the fallen with a tender and redeeming hand.

JESUS AND THE TWO SISTERS

With its mingling of sickness and pain, love and trust, sorrow and death, resurrection and life, the eleventh chapter of John is one of the most heart-moving in the New Testament. All the recorded incidents in it revolve around the close-knit family in Bethany—the spiritual retreat of Jesus. At the age of thirty, he left the Nazareth home in which he grew up, and we have no record of his returning to it during his brief ministry. When by "thronging duties pressed" and in need of relaxation, Jesus found his way to the home of three unmarried friends whom he had come to love. Of the happy association of Jesus with Mary, Martha, and Lazarus in Bethany, F. B. Meyer says in his *Commentary on John:*

> Their home was the one green oasis in the rugged wilderness through which he passed to his Cross; we think of the pure and holy love that broke in upon his loneliness and the true affection that softened the bitterness of his last days, so far at least as human love could.

In this ideal home Jesus found the curse of the sojourner lifted from him, and, in reversal of his own description of his loneliness and penury, found where to lay his head.

The chapter, as a whole, will ever be counted precious since it is saturated with tears, including those Jesus himself shed. In *Commentary on the New Testament* F. Godet says of the chapter that "no scene in the Gospel of John is presented in so detailed and dramatic manner as we find here. There is none from which appears more distinctly the character of Jesus as at once perfectly Divine and perfectly human, and none which more fully justifies the central declaration of the Prologue: *The Word was made flesh.*" As the man Christ Jesus, he wept; as God manifest in flesh, he said to a corpse, "Come forth, and he that was dead came forth" (John 11:35, 43, 44). What a striking combination of tears and triumph, pain and power!

We can also note in passing that Mary, Martha, and Lazarus are the only persons *named* in the

Gospels as being loved by Jesus (John 11:5). John was far too modest to name himself as "the disciple whom Jesus loved" (John 13:23; 21:20, 24). The term used for *loved* is the nobler, more dignified one than that used as an expression of tenderness, appropriate in the mouth of the sisters as they thought of their affection for the Master. The tears of Jesus reveal the loving, tender sympathy he had for the grief of the two sisters and of others mourning the death of Lazarus. One does not raise the dead with a heart of stone. Those tears of his—liquid pain—were not for Lazarus, for one does not weep over a beloved friend whom he will soon see again.

The two sisters, Martha and Mary, were corecipients of divine love, cosufferers in sickness and death, and coparticipants in the miraculous power of the friend who had loved them both (John 11:17–33; Luke 10:38–42). Both of these passages portray the two women as being possessed of the same characteristics, surely an undesigned coincidence affirming a proof of genuineness. The two sisters, so different, as we shall see, were yet each so devoted to Jesus and so confident of his love and power that they stand out among the most interesting characters in John's Gospel. And knowing that they were not on a lower plane than men either spiritually or intellectually, Jesus opened up for Martha and Mary deep wells of truth.

"Men have different gifts, but it is the same Spirit Who gives them. There are different ways of serving God, but it is the same Lord Who is served" (1 Cor. 12:4, 5, Phillips). Paul makes it clear that there is great variety among the Lord's people and that it is evidently not the design of grace to make them all alike as the natural, opposite characteristics of Martha and Mary prove. What marked diversities there were in that Bethany home! The two sisters and their brother were not like peas in a pod, but so different. Yet Jesus loved them each with all their personal, peculiar traits for in the opening of this marvelous chapter is written the affirmation, "Jesus loved Martha, and her sister, and Lazarus."

The fact is evident that the sisters were one in concern for their sick brother and in their faith that the friend who loved them was able to help. While they looked to him for sympathy, they did not ask for it. They felt it was enough to tell him of their trial and then leave the matter with him. "His sisters sent unto him, saying, Lord, behold, he whom thou lovest is sick." These dear women of Bethany had confidence in the continuance of Jesus' love, hence, the present tense *lovest,* not past tense *lovedst.*

To such an affectionate and urgent request, Jesus sent a somewhat puzzling reply. He said that Lazarus would die but that death would not be the end of the sickness laying him low. The tears of Martha and Mary would give luster to the jewels of the crown of Jesus as he proved himself to be the victor over death in the resurrection of Lazarus for the glory of God. What perplexed the sisters still further was the delay of Jesus in coming to the help of the man he loved. They had hastened in sending him tidings of the sickness of Lazarus, but he manifested no haste to come to him. "He abode two days still in the same place where he was." Conscious he was God, and able to cope with the situation, Jesus was in no hurry. He sought to teach Martha and Mary that his delays are not denials, that although he may appear to tarry, he is never too late. In any need that may arise we can with confidence wait for him (Heb. 10:37). To quote F. B. Meyer again:

> To the sisters he must have appeared neglectful but he was not really so . . . The whole situation was constantly present to him, till he saw that he could interpose with the best possible result. So is it ever. His step may linger; but his watchful interest never falters. There is not a sigh, a pang, a tear, that escapes his notice. There is not a fluttering pulse which he does not feel, noticing its tremulous anxiety. He *sits* as a refiner of silver. He knows our sorrows, and is acquainted with our grief. He slumbers not, nor sleeps.

As to the personal characteristics of the two sisters, the record reveals them to be totally different in temperament. Yet theirs was a diversity in unity.

Mary was meditative and reticent, tender and clinging, and gifted with all a woman's delicacy of insight and loving sympathy. She thought little about necessary housework, being unwilling to lose a minute of the precious company of him at whose feet she could sit in silence and rest in his wonderful presence.

Martha, on the other hand, was somewhat impulsive and active, practical, businesslike, abounding in energy, revealing her love by making every preparation, executive and efficient, determined that nothing should lack in the entertainment of the friend she loved. She typifies the strong housewife ever thoughtful of all concerning the comfort and well-being of those for whom she feels responsible. Yet Jesus loved both sisters.

It must not be felt for one moment, however, that Martha was all movement and no meditation, for Luke has the delightful touch, "Martha . . .

had a sister called Mary, which *also* sat at Jesus' feet, and heard his word" (Luke 10:39). So both had tuition in the College of the Feet, but Martha felt that home duties must have some of her time, as well as the spiritual luxury of receiving divine instruction. As for Mary, she had little thought of home service, so long as she could be with her friend. Somehow she felt that he would rather have *her* than the things she could do for him. This is not to say that Jesus did not fail to see that Martha was likewise expressing her devotion in her own way. In his loving rebuke, did he not imply that her fussiness for things mattered little; that what he wanted in the way of hospitality was simplest fare and, above all, *herself*? Jesus loved both of these fine women, not for what they could do for his comfort so much as for the spiritual intercourse he ever sought in the home.

Jesus taught that the one thing most needful in life was fellowship with himself and that this was the good part Mary had chosen and must be nurtured (Luke 10:42). It was Martha not Mary, however, who received from Jesus the most notable and astounding declaration, "I am the resurrection and the life." Hers was the quiet complaint when Jesus ultimately appeared for the burial of Lazarus that had he come sooner he could have prevented her brother's death. Yet she believed that he could secure his resurrection at "the last day" about which Jesus often spoke (John 6:44, 45). But as she was joyfully to experience, the raising of her brother was not to be a far-off event, for the Master said, "I am myself the resurrection." How positive and comprehensive was her reply to the question of Jesus, "Believest thou this?" Without hesitation she replied, "Yea, Lord: I believe that thou art the Christ, the Son of God, which should come into the world" (John 11:26, 27).

When Mary heard from Martha about Jesus' arrival, she "arose quickly" and came to him, expressing, thereby, the eagerness of heart's affection for him. How Mary illustrated that the chariot wheels of love fly swiftly round!

> 'Tis love that makes our willing feet
> In swift obedience move.

Taking up her accustomed place at the feet of Jesus (Luke 10:39; John 11:32), Mary confronted him with the same complaint as Martha, "Lord, if thou hadst been here my brother had not died." Evidently the two sisters had agreed on this matter and up to this point exhibited the same character of faith, but in other respects the faith of Martha was in advance of Mary. Still, the tears of Mary over the death of her brother, as well as the tears of the friends with her, moved, most deeply, the heart of Jesus who, whenever he saw a funeral, upset it and raised the dead. So we have the shortest text in the Bible—*Jesus wept!* The Jews felt that his warm tears were the expression of his love for a much-loved friend whom death had robbed. How touched he ever is with the feeling of our infirmities! Says Hugh Macmillan, "It is the Christian religion alone that reveals to us a God of tears."

Well, as we know, the miracle happened, and Jesus raised the one intimate male friend he possessed outside the circles of the apostles—a miracle that made many Jews turn and believe in Jesus (John 11:45). After this most important and striking, in many respects, of all the miracles of Jesus, he left Bethany for Ephraim (John 11:54) but returned a week later when, in his honor and to celebrate the resurrection of Lazarus, a supper was planned in the home he dearly loved. Martha, practical as ever, served (John 12:1–11). In the previous chapter, Bethany was "the town of Mary and her sister Martha," but now it is the place "where Lazarus was which had been dead, but whom Jesus raised from the dead" (John 12:1). How true it is that in a wonderful way Jesus leaves his mark on all the places and hearts he visits (John 12:9).

That celebration-supper will ever be memorable because of Mary's love-gift to Jesus for his power in calling her beloved brother from the grave. The strong pure love of her heart felt there was no gift too costly for him who was about to die himself and rise from the grave. In fact, Jesus said that Mary had intended the most expensive ointment she had anointed his feet with, to anoint his body on the day of burial (John 12:7). Judas felt that the large amount of money which the gift cost Mary, who was by no means wealthy, had been wasted, or that her money should have been better spent by giving it to the poor. But Jesus saw behind the act of Mary in anointing his feet the intensity of love and that any idea of rebuff to such a gift of gratitude and devotion would be utterly repugnant.

Jesus loved Mary, but the love was not one-sided, and the grateful sister gave to the limit out of an overflowing heart of love. Regardless of cost, love must express itself and approve itself by deeds. Thus the love of Mary justified itself in the eyes of love—his love—which ever kindles love. Wherever the gospel of him who is "the resurrection and the life" has been preached, Mary's deed has been proclaimed with it, stirring the hearts of men and women to yield themselves and their substance to him who broke his box of spikenard very costly at Calvary. Have you brought him your alabaster box, and has the breaking of it filled your home and the hearts and lives of others with the perfume of the sacrifice?

Selfishness seeks a gift,
  Love loves to give;
Giving itself away
  Love loves to live.

Love's grand munificence
  Counts not the cost;
Feeling, though nought is left,
  Nothing is lost.

JESUS AND THE WOMAN TAKEN IN ADULTERY

The record John gives us of this profligate woman has been the subject of more eager debate than any other in the Gospels. In fact, the margin of the Revised Version notes: "Most of the ancient authorities omit, John 7:53–8:11." Even Bishop Westcott says, "The evidence against the genuineness of the woman take in adultery, John 8:1–11, as an original piece of the Gospel—both external and internal—is overwhelming." He goes on to say what other scholars affirm that the incident is "beyond doubt an authentic fragment of apostolic tradition."

But John himself gave the narrative his sanction, as did the early church, and the account of the woman is in every particular so like other contacts of Jesus that there is nothing in the presentation of this degraded female which would lead us to doubt its authenticity (see Luke 7:36–50). We heartily agree with the conclusion of Dean Farrar that "Were the critical evidence against the genuineness of this passage far more overwhelming than it is, the story would yet bear upon its surface the strongest possible proof of its own truthfulness." Meyer's *Commentary on John* captions this portion "The Penitent's Gospel," and states:

> There is no possibility of accounting for its existence, save on the supposition that the incident really took place. It reveals in our Saviour's character a wisdom so profound, a tenderness to sinners so delicate, a hatred of sin so intense, an insight into human hearts so searching, that it is impossible to suppose the mind of man could have conceived, or the hand of man invented, this most pathetic story.

The characters portrayed by John are the scribes and the Pharisees, the woman guilty of flagrant sin, and Jesus, who by his actions and words teaches us many precious lessons.

The scribes and Pharisees and Jesus. After spending a night on the Mount of Olives, Jesus came to the Temple and, drawing a seat against the treasury wall, sat down and began to teach those who gathered to hear him. But before he had gone too far in his message, a company of his persistent foes, "adorned with their customary badges of sanctity," interrupted his discourse by placing before him a trembling, shrinking woman who had been caught in the act of adultery; they demanded what should be done with her. This was a shameful plot on their part in order to trap Jesus, and some writers suggest that one reason

Jesus stooped down to write on the ground was to conceal the burning shame and holy indignation that leapt to his face over the detestable actions of those scribes and Pharisees.

These "self-appointed inspectors of moral nuisances," who regarded themselves as custodians of public morality, and who regarded publicans and sinners with sanctimonious contempt, were guilty of the very sin for which they desired to have the woman judged. Cowardlike, they brought *a woman,* not the man guilty of abusing her. The Law of Moses, on which the Pharisees prided themselves as being authorities, required that both the adulterer and the adulteress should be judged and put to death (Lev. 20:10). Why, then, was the adulterer not brought to Jesus as well? Why was the woman brought alone as if she were the chief sinner—the one sinning rather than sinned against? Can it be that the adulterer was a Pharisee, one of the company of the accusers, and that policy required that he should not be exposed? Their judgment of the woman was not "without partiality" (James 3:17).

Further, nothing could have been more cruel or harsh than the publicity those Pharisees exposed that weak woman to as they set her "in the midst" of all who were gathered around Jesus. While justice demands the exposure of the guilt of sinners, it is the very nature of love to shield them from public gaze (1 Pet. 4:8). Thus, as Dean Farrar expresses it, "Their conduct showed on their parts a cold, hard cynicism, a graceless, pitiless, barbarous brutality of heart and conscience." These heartless men, clad in the robes of virtuous horror, were incapable of measuring the anguish of the sin-stained heart of the woman they had dragged before Jesus.

Truly, it is a sorry state of things when a sinner falls into the hand of fellow sinners whose sin has blinded them to their own faults and sharpens their detection of the sins of others. Those Pharisees took a prurient pleasure in enumerating all the details—*in the very act.* They held the sinful woman up as a public spectacle—setting *her in the midst*—and left her to her fate which, according to the Law, was death by stoning. Testing Jesus, the Pharisees brought him face to face with the Law of Moses and said, "The law commanded us, that such should be stoned: but what sayest thou" (John 8:5)? They appealed to Moses because he represented a standard Jesus himself regarded and honored (Ps. 40:8). Previously, Jesus had said that Moses was the accuser of the scribes and Pharisees, and it was therefore strange that in accusing the woman they should appeal to Moses (John 5:45).

But the Law could not forgive the woman and transform her life. All it could do was to condemn and demand punishment for sin. The Law of Moses was framed for the purpose of dealing with sin *judicially.* Tenderness and clemency it did not countenance, for in its austerity it implied

> —and in the course of justice none of us
> Should see salvation.

The Law, as an executioner, is commissioned to do its work; and "the offender falls beneath its curse and penalty." Meyer further says:

> The function of the Law is two-fold. *First* it has to reveal our need of salvation; to hold up the looking-glass that we may go for soap; to convince of our disease that we may hasten for the physician; to make

us feel the badness of our best till we are shut in Christ. *Next,* it has to smite, and scourge, and punish us, when we go aside from the narrow thread-like path of perfect goodness. The sinner therefore has no hope as he stands beneath Mount Sinai. He cannot climb those cliffs. Nay, he is smitten down by the pieces of the broken tables as they leap downwards from crag to crag. And Moses, with one blow of his fist, so John Bunyan tells us, completes the work.

Jesus and the woman. In the second part of the story we breathe purer air. There stood the woman before Jesus, not of her free will. She had been forced, ashamed and unresisting, to appear before Jesus as a judge of morals, but she came to know him as the lover of her soul. The exposure of her sin by her accusers led to the remedy for her sin in Jesus. How the delicacy of Jesus shines forth in his treatment of this degraded woman! The Pharisees, after presenting their case against her, asked Jesus, "What sayest thou?" but he said nothing, no reply to the Pharisees, no word of condemnation for the sinner. We have the dramatic, expressive silence of Jesus: "But Jesus stooped down, and with his finger wrote on the ground, *as though he had heard them not.*"

Why did Jesus wait before uttering the words of peace the sinful woman needed to hear? Why he stooped to write in the dust at his feet, and what he wrote, we are not told. If what he wrote was legible, did the adulteress read it and gain life? Many are the reasons conjectured for the action of Jesus in stooping and looking down. One reason is that his pure nature shrunk from gazing at the guilty woman who had been dragged into his presence. Men of corrupt hearts, "having eyes full of adultery" (2 Pet. 2:14), as the Pharisees had, might stare at her, but the holy, loving, compassionate Jesus must look another way.

Another conjectured reason for his downward look is that he wanted to reflect upon the holiness of the divine law. He could not condone the woman's sin. She had broken the Law, and he must honor it. It may be that he paused to say anything that his treatment of her might be delayed. Righteous wrath must have been his over the hard, callous, supercilious attitude of the Pharisees, but Jesus was "slow to anger" even though they kept on asking him for an answer to their question. Little did those loveless, pitiless accusers realize that the averted face of Jesus would make them bow their heads in shame, as conscience-stricken they slunk away, crushed by his simple yet piercing words.

Lifting his head, his first word was not for the sinner trembling before him but for the Pharisees, and how it stung them—"He that is without sin among you, let him first cast a stone" (John 8:7). When Jesus said "without sin," he meant the particular sin of adultery of which the Pharisees condemned the woman, caught in the act, to be guilty. He determined that no stone must be thrown at her save by those who were innocent of the sin with which she was charged. The only one in the group that day who was perfectly holy, and therefore "without sin," was Jesus, but he lifted no stone against the defenseless woman.

The shaft went home and, "convicted by their own conscience, went out one by one, *beginning at the eldest,* even unto the last." The phrase, "beginning at the *eldest,*" speaks volumes. In spite of his seniority, he was exposed as an adulterer himself. Says Matthew Henry, "They that are convicted by their own consciences, will be condemned by their Judge if they are not acquitted by their Redeemer. Had those Pharisees stayed there might have been a further revelation of their guilt." But if that mysterious writing on the ground was a record of the iniquity of which they knew they were guilty, then we can understand their humiliating retreat from the presence of the thrice holy one.

The second time Jesus stooped down and wrote on the ground represented another dramatic pause before he dealt with the woman; and seeing no other, he asked, "Woman, where are those thine accusers? Hath no man . . .? She said, No man, Lord" (John 8:10). She might have fled when her convicted accusers did, but she was constrained to remain with the one she had come to see had the only right to judge her. The Pharisees cried, "Stone her." Somewhere she felt Jesus was there to "save her," which he did, for he was not there as a judge and therefore passed no sentence. If the Pharisees could not condemn her, how could he? So the heart of the woman taken in adultery was strangely warmed as she heard her deliverer say, "Neither do I condemn thee: go, and sin no more." Jesus would not have used the words, *sin no more,* if she had not been guilty. In his contacts with women, there were at least three who had been guilty of adultery—the woman of Samaria, the woman who came to him in Simon's house, and the woman we have been considering. Loving-kindness and tender mercy characterized his dealings with each of them. "Go, and sin no more." This last word of Jesus is in perfect agreement with his blessed purpose to save sinners, even the most degraded and the most disgraced.

How full of encouragement this story is for the fallen womanhood of our day! For the crushed and sinning all around us, it offers a ground of hope and an assurance that there is a heart that cares. For women, sinning and sinned against, and generally condemned, what a new world opens when they hear and respond to the Savior's message of forgiveness and warning, "Neither do I condemn thee: go, and sin no more."

> His blood can make the vilest clean,
> His blood avails for me.

JESUS AND THE DAUGHTERS OF JERUSALEM

We cannot think of any other great religious teacher whose contacts with women were so full of meaning and formed so important a part of his life as the one "born of a woman." There was something dynamic in his treatment of women, and the place of women in the world's life and their rights in social and family life have been won largely through those who have caught the spirit of Jesus. We have only to think of the plight of women in those lands where his redeeming Gospel has not penetrated to appreciate what those who are not the mere slaves of the passion of men owe to his ennobling influence.

Among the honorable women Jesus encountered in the days of his flesh were those he named "Daughters of Jerusalem" (Luke 23:27–31) and to whom he had some striking things to say. Among the great company of people following Jesus to Calvary was a group of women who also bewailed and lamented him. It has been suggested that these devout women formed one of the sisterhoods in Jerusalem whose gracious task was the mitigation of the sufferings of condemned criminals by narcotic drinks. Mary and Martha may have been among the sorrowful women accompanying Jesus to Calvary.

How characteristic it was of the Master to bury his own sorrow in the thought of others who wept and mourned. The tenderness of our Lord's sympathy can be seen in these first words coming from his lips after he left the presence of Pilate. The mocking, the scourging, the spitting had all been borne in silence. Now he speaks and his thoughts are of the far-off sufferings of others, rather than those that were then falling upon himself. What tenderness there is in his message to the female sympathizers. "Weep not for me, but weep for yourselves, and for your children." He himself had wept over the sinners in Jerusalem (Luke 19:41); now he urges the women not to weep for him, not that it was wrong of them to show their sympathy, but to weep for a far greater reason, namely, the destruction of their city and the overthrow of their nation, which took place when the Romans ravished Jerusalem and slew its inhabitants. The beatitude of Jesus, "Blessed are the barren," implies that women with no children, during the siege of the city, were spared the horrors of seeing children slain, as so many fond mothers witnessed.

Jesus predicted that the great calamities and judgments about to overtake the city and its people would cause them to cry out for shelter and for the hills to cover them. The same figure is used of the godless in tribulation judgment (Rev.

6:16, 17). Then the metaphor Jesus used of "the green tree" is a proverbial expression calling for an explanation. "If they [Roman powers] do these things in a green tree, what shall be done in the dry" (Luke 23:31)? Barnes' *Notes on the New Testament* has this satisfying interpretation:

> A green tree is one that is not easily set on fire. A dry one is easily kindled, and burns rapidly. By a green tree is represented, evidently, a man of truth and purity. And the meaning of the passage is: "If they, the Romans, do these things to me, who am innocent and blameless—if they punish me in this manner in the face of justice—what will they not do in relation to this guilty nation? What security have they that heavier judgments will not come upon them? What desolations and woes may not be expected when injustice and oppression have taken the place of justice, and have set up a rule over this wicked people?" Thus applied, the proverb means that the sufferings of the Saviour, compared with the sufferings of the guilty, were like the burning of a green tree compared with the burning of one that is dry. A green tree is not adapted to burn; a dry one is. So the Saviour—innocent, pure, and holy—stood in relation to suffering. . . . The sinner is adapted to sufferings—like a dry tree is to the fire. Guilty, he suffers all the horrors of remorse of conscience.

JESUS AND MARY MAGDALENE

As Luke is preeminently the "Gospel of Womanhood" because of the many figuring in the life of Jesus, so John stands out as the "Gospel of Conversations" since it gives more largely than the other Gospels the individualism of Jesus as expressed in his interviews. John records twenty-four conversations held with seventeen different people. These conversations were often brief monologues of Jesus, and some were directions for his miracles. Conspicuous among his personal talks is the contact with Mary Magdalene in the garden, just after he had risen from the dead (John 20:11–18).

Are you not impressed by the fact that the only friends to stand by Jesus in the closing scenes of his life were *women?* His disciples forsook him and fled, but the women remained near him with tortured hearts, being unable to leave him alone in his terrible plight. They ministered unto him of more than their substance, for as the curtain falls, the small band of loyal and loving women are there, standing by the cross. They were the last to leave the grim spot and the first at his tomb after his burial. And how eloquent are his few words of his relation to them. They had been his friends, bringing him much comfort and strength in his life of strenuous service for others, and they were faithful to the end.

We learn that the encounter with Mary Magdalene was his first appearance after he arose from the dead (Mark 16:9–11). Peter and John and the other women had left the garden tomb where the body of Jesus lay, but Mary Magdalene remained there alone, weeping her heart out for him to whom she owed so much. Even when the angel announced to her that Jesus had risen, the good news did not seem to register. Grief numbed her senses for a few moments. With the rest of the disciples she had heard Jesus say repeatedly that he would rise the third day, but somehow his declaration was not understood. Well, he had gone, and she thought his body had been stolen as she gazed at the empty tomb and begged the angels to tell her where that precious body had gone.

Then it happened. Turning around, she saw Jesus standing, but she knew not that he was the one she loved so much and over whom she had shed so many tears. Then he said to Mary, "Why weepest thou? Whom seekest thou?" It would seem as if Jesus disguised his voice a little to lead her on, for she supposed the speaker to be the gardener who had transferred the body of Jesus to another tomb. How pathetic her plea—"Tell me where thou hast laid him, and I will take him away"! What utter devotion such a plea reveals! But then Jesus uttered only one word in a voice that could not be mistaken—*Mary!* She recognized the tender tone and cried out in ecstatic joy, *Rabboni!* which means "master" (see John 20:16, R.V.). It was not an occasion for many words. "There are spiritual experiences that almost deprive men of the power of utterance, and all they can do is to wonder and adore." It was so with Mary.

Later on, Jesus appeared to the other women (Matt. 28:9–10), but Mary was the first to see him, alive forevermore. The well-loved inflection of the Master's voice opened her eyes, enabling her to see that wonder of all wonders, Jesus alive whom she last saw dead upon the cross. His further words to Mary have received various interpretations, but the simplest explanation of them is that Mary, in her exuberance, tried to detain Jesus. But he meant, "Do not detain me now: for I am not yet ascended to my Father and your Father, and to my God and your God" (20:17). Pause over the phrase, *my Father and your Father*, for in it Jesus identified himself with Mary and Mary with himself. Both had an eternal relationship with the Father. Following the command of her Lord, Mary went and told the disciples the glorious news, and although a woman, became the first herald of the resurrection. How privileged she was!

A concluding word is necessary as to who Mary Magdalene actually was. She is named more than any of the other women who followed Jesus, and usually first; she was the outstanding leader of them (see Matt. 27:56, 61; 28:1; Mark 15:40, 47; 16:1, 9; Luke 8:2; 24:10; John 19:25; 20:1, 18). Named among the women who ministered unto Jesus of their substance, she was evidently a woman of wealth. The label she wore was, "Out of whom went seven devils." But this is no indication that she was unchaste or like the sinful woman Luke describes (Luke 7:36–50). Nowhere is Mary Magdalene associated with human immorality. In this respect she has been maligned, for, in the past, homes and institutes for prostitutes and fallen women have been given the name of *Magdalene,* inferring thereby that she was a woman of shame whom Jesus rescued. It is unthinkable that Jesus would accept such a woman as the leader among the women who followed him. When demons invaded human beings, they caused sickness and disease of various kinds, and it was in this way Mary had been afflicted (Mark 5:1–20). The sacred record stamps her as a woman of unblemished character and worthy of the honor of being the first to proclaim, *He is risen!* Says Sibbes, "A woman is sent to be the apostle to the Apostles."

BIBLE STUDY QUESTIONS

Take time to turn to each Scripture reference and mark the verse or a portion in your Bible.

1. How did Jesus' regard for women contrast with Roman law?
2. Describe how Jesus regarded widows.
3. What are some of the lessons learned from Jesus, Mary, and Martha?
4. How did Jesus show love to the woman taken in adultery?
5. In what way was Mary Magdalene made a leader of the disciples?

—7—

About Children

When the Lord of glory became the holy child Jesus, he entered into a personal experience of a child's nature and needs; thus his mandate is as clear as it is challenging, "Suffer the little children to come unto me, and forbid them not: for of such is the kingdom of God." "The babe wrapped in swaddling clothes, lying in a manger" was a sign that there had been "born in the city of David a Saviour, which is Christ the Lord" (Luke 2:11). Gabriel referred to the royal babe as *that holy thing,* an expression never applied to any other child in all the world save Mary's child. Alexander Whyte says in *Walk, Conversation, and Character of Jesus Christ Our Lord:*

> It is a very startling, and indeed staggering expression to be found applied to her Child, to hear him called that *thing,* even when it is added, that *holy* thing. But the evangelist's so startling expression has the seal of the Holy Ghost upon it . . . Human nature in all its stages and in all its conditions is a very wonderful thing. But as soon as the *thing* we call human nature is taken up into himself by a person, that human nature is no longer a mere thing. . . . In like

manner, when "that holy thing," which was conceived by the power of the Holy Ghost in the womb of the Virgin Mary, was taken up into himself by the Son of God, that holy thing henceforward and for ever becomes and abides part and parcel of the Son of God.

Many poets wrote feelingly about the nativity. In the sixteenth century, Richard Crashaw wrote:

> Gloomy night embrac'd the place
> Where the noble Infant lay.
> The Babe look't up and shew'd his face;
> In spite of darkness, it was day.
> It was Thy day, sweet! and did rise
> Not from the East, but from thine eyes.

Then in his "Hymn on the Morning of Christ's Nativity," John Milton says:

> It was the winter wild
> While the heaven-born Child
> All meanly wrapt in the rude manger lies;
> Nature in awe to Him
> Had doff't her gaudy trim,
> With her great Master so to sympathize.

C. F. Alexander, who wrote many of our well-known hymns, gave us this Christmas one:

> Once in royal David's city
>   Stood a lowly cattle shed,
> Where a Mother laid her Baby
>   In a manger for His bed:
> Mary was that Mother mild,
> Jesus Christ her little child.

Children love to hear and read about his birth and childhood because

> He's a Friend for little children,
> Above the bright, blue sky.

C. G. Alexander further expresses this thought.

For, He is our childhood's pattern,
  Day by day like us He grew,
He was little, weak, and helpless,
  Tears and smiles like us He knew;
And He feeleth for our sadness,
And He shareth in our gladness.

Then there are the appealing lines of Bishop Heber:

O Thou, Whose infant feet were found
  Within Thy Father's shrine,
Whose years, with changeless virtue crowned,
  Were all alike Divine;
Dependent on Thy bounteous breath,
  We seek Thy grace alone,
In Childhood, Manhood, Age and Death,
  To keep us still Thine own!

As God ordained marriage for the creation of children, let us begin by examining the *value* Scripture places upon them. Says the psalmist, "Children are an heritage of the Lord. . . . Happy is the man that hath his quiver full of them" (Ps. 127:1–5). The truly happy home is the one where children are like "olive branches round about the table" (Ps. 128:3). Wordsworth in his "Ode: Intimations of Immortality" reminds us:

But trailing clouds of glory do we come
  From God, who is our home:
Heaven lies about us in our infancy!

As for Tennyson, he would have us know that the ideal home is one in which can be found "Household happiness, gracious children, debtless competence, golden mean." Of old, the firstborn son was claimed as Jehovah's and dedicated to him. Thus Mary brought Jesus, her firstborn, to the Temple. Throughout Scripture, the gift of a son from Jehovah was the height of joy; the loss of a child marked the depth of woe (Gen. 21:16; 33:5; Job 29:5; Matt. 19:13; Luke 2:48, etc.). It was because children were regarded as divine gifts, pledges of God's favor (Gen. 4:1; 33:5), that barrenness was deemed a reproach, a divine punishment involving disgrace in the eyes in the world (Gen. 16:4; 30:1). This is why Elizabeth rejoiced when the Lord took away her "reproach among men" (Luke 1:25), and Jesus referred to the joy of a woman at the birth of a child into the world (John 16:21).

But although children are divine gifts, after they enter the world, their spiritual and moral development depends upon the atmosphere of the home in which they find themselves. Many who heard of the birth of John the Baptist asked, "What manner of child shall this be?" His growth in grace, however, was assured, not only because of his saintly parents, but because "the hand of the Lord was with him" (Luke 1:66). Elizabeth and Zacharias fulfilled the admonition of Sir H. Baker, centuries before he was born.

> O ye who came that Babe to lay
> Within a Saviour's arms to-day,
> Watch well the guard with careful eye,
> The Heir of Immortality.

A prayer used in the Anglican church at the consecration service of children reads,

> Grant, we beseech Thee, O Lord, that this child may hereafter not be ashamed to confess the faith of Christ crucified, and manfully to fight under His ban-

ner against sin, the World, and the Devil, and to continue Christ's faithful soldier and servant unto his (or her) life's end.

PARENTS AND CHILDREN

Whether from the cradle of an infant there grows a child of God or a child of the Devil depends to a very large degree upon the quality of the home and the training received. Solomon, who in *Proverbs* has a great deal to say about children, wrote, "Train up a child in the way he should go: and when he is old, he will not depart from it" (Prov. 22:6). The standard of family life develops or degrades a child. Great, then, is the responsibility of parents, especially mothers, from whom naturally children receive their first lessons. Ancient Jews regarded the education of a child as a religious duty in itself and to be discharged with the religious purpose of bringing him up in the fear of the Lord.

The home in which Jesus was born was poor but *pious,* and he found himself in an environment in harmony with his holiness as "the holy thing" born of Mary, from whom he would be taught the Old Testament before he was old enough to go to the village synagogue school. When, ultimately, Jesus entered his public ministry, he illustrated in his teaching the relation of father and child in its affection and authority (Luke 11:11, 12; Matt. 21:28–31). Further he upheld the paramount duty of the fifth commandment. "Honour thy father and thy mother [against the tradition of the elders]" (Mark 7:9–13). Jesus also set all children an example by his own conduct while at home in which he was subject to his parents (Luke 2:51). He lived out the apostolic injunction, "Children, obey your parents in the Lord: for this is right" (Eph. 6:1). We catch many glimpses in his teaching of experiences and scenes he observed as a growing child.

Alexander Whyte concludes chapter two of his volume with this appeal to parents:

> Pray importunately that your child also may be made of God, both to him, and to you, a twin-brother of the Holy Child Jesus. Pray without ceasing that your child may be sanctified with the self-same sanctification as Mary's Child. And if that may not be perfected all at once, as his sanctification was, pray that at least it may be begun as long as you are here to see it and to have a hand in it. Take your child apart, as long as he is docile and will go with you, and ask on your knees, and in his hearing something like this—
>
> "O God, the God and Father of the Holy Child Jesus, make this, my dear child, a child of God like him. And after I am gone make him and keep him a man of God like him."
>
> Take no rest to yourself, and give God no rest, till you see a seed of God not only sown in your child's heart, but till you see him, as Mary saw her first-born Son, subject to her in everything in her house at home, and growing up every day in wisdom, and in stature, and in favour with God and man.

JESUS AND CHILDREN—MIRACLES

No one can meditate upon Jesus' contacts with children and his teaching concerning them without coming to the conclusion that he had a deep affection for the young. The simple chorus children of today often sing is true of him who came as the personification of divine love for old and young alike.

> Jesus loves the little children,
> All the children of the world,
> Red and yellow, black and white,
> All are precious in his sight.
> Jesus loves the children of the world.

This is why they were, and are, instinctively drawn to him. The native innocency, simplicity, and artlessness of children make it easy for them to believe the stories of Jesus. Their minds are not lumbered with the doubts and questions affecting more adult minds and thus decision to love the Savior comes without effort as they learn to sing:

> Gentle Jesus, meek and mild,
> Look upon a little child;
> Pity my simplicity,
> Suffer me to come to Thee.

First, let us think of his contacts with children, especially those who figure in his miracles. Jesus was always deeply moved when he encountered human suffering, particularly in the young through no fault of their own. Some of his most pungent sayings arose out of his miracles. Those wrought on children were accompanied by exquisite touches of humanity toward the parents.

Nobleman's son (John 4:46–54). John says that this healing of the nobleman's son was "again the second miracle that Jesus did" (John 4:54). This does not mean his miracle in the turning of water into wine in Cana (John 2:1–12). After this, Jesus performed many miracles elsewhere, but he "came again into Cana of Galilee" out of

Judea (John 4:46, 54); thus the healing of the sick boy was his second miracle in Cana. The reputation and influence of his first miracle in Cana lingered on, and as soon as the nobleman heard that Jesus was back in Galilee, he sought the aid of Jesus for his dying son, believing that if he could change water into best wine, he could transform a very sick child into a healthy one.

But when the distressed father and Jesus met, the reply given to the request for Jesus to come to the home and heal the child appears perplexing. "Except ye see signs and wonders, ye will not believe" (John 4:48). This cannot mean that the man would not believe in the power of Jesus to restore his child until the miracle actually happened. The very fact that he came with haste to Jesus for help as soon as he heard that he was back in Galilee was surely an evidence that he believed Jesus was able to stay the hand of death. "Sir, come down ere my child die." What is implied in the reply of Jesus is his reflection on the man's request. "If ye see, ye will believe." The man had not thought that the physical presence in the sick chamber was not necessary to performance of the miracle requested.

Thus, the response of Jesus actually meant that unless he personally went to the sick child, and the father saw with his own eyes the healing sought, he would not believe. But he felt that the remark of Jesus was not an answer, and consequently not a refusal, and so renewed his request, making it more touching but using a term of affection, "Come down ere *my child* die." Godet says that in the granting of the request by Jesus there was also a partial refusal, which was a test.

Jesus yields to the faith which breathes in the prayer, but in such a way as immediately to elevate faith to a higher degree. "Go thy way, thy son liveth." The healing is granted: but without Jesus leaving Cana; he wishes this time to be believed on his word. Until now the father had believed on the testimony of others. Now his faith is to rest on a better support, on the personal contact which he has just had with the Lord himself.

On his way home, the nobleman met his servants and was greeted with the good news, "Thy son liveth." Faith had been rewarded, for the father "believed the word that Jesus had spoken unto him." Inquiring of his servants about the hour his boy began to mend, the father was told "the seventh hour." He remembered that that was "the same hour in which Jesus said unto him, 'Thy son liveth,' " and learned how Jesus could heal by remote control—a divine ability the centurion recognized when, meeting Jesus, he said, "Speak the word only, and my servant shall be healed." Reaching home he found that his servant was healed the very hour Jesus said, "Go thy way; and as thou hast believed, so be it done unto thee" (Matt. 8:5–13).

The Syrophoenician's daughter (Matt. 15:21–28; Mark 7:24–30). This further miracle bringing relief to the daughter of a woman of Canaan affords another instance of an occasion providing Jesus with the opportunity of uttering some startling truths. First, when he sent his disciples forth, it was with the precept, "Go not into the way of the Gentiles," yet here he is heading in the direction of Tyre. Why did he go? Mark tells us that it was partly because of rest (Mark 7:24) and, as the narrative shows, partly because a soul desired mercy. Because of his omniscience, Jesus knew that his rest would be invaded by the Gentile woman of Canaan.

Evidently a change had come over this heathen worshiper of Ashtoreth, or "Queen of Heaven," prayers to whom for her demon-vexed child fell on dead ears. It would seem as if the distressed mother was a widow, and the fear of losing her daughter after her husband's death filled her with despair, seeing intercession to the goddess was unavailing. Some from Tyre and Sidon had seen Jesus and been healed by him (Luke 6:17); so she made her way to him, calling, "Lord, thou son of David." Afflicted people reason very boldly, and this Gentile woman with a broken heart cried to Jesus the Jew, reverently and lovingly, "My daughter is grievously vexed with a devil." Believing him to be "a very present help in trouble," she pleads for mercy. But alas! her faith and plea were not at once successful.

It seemed as if her prayer to the living God had fallen upon deaf ears, just as her cries had upon the dead ears of the "Queen of Heaven," for we read, "Jesus answered her not a word." But, as she was to learn to her joy, his failure to respond was not rejection of her plea. The disciples besought Jesus to grant the desperate woman her wish and send her away, to which came his reply, crushing though it might have been to a Gentile mother pleading for her child, "I am not sent but unto the lost sheep of the house of Israel." The loving face of Jesus may have seemed to contradict his silence, but he has more reasons for silence than we think. The psalmist cried, "Be not silent unto me," but divine silence is always golden in its purpose, as the distraught mother was to prove. Jesus had not come seeking her; she sought him and, prostrating herself before him, cried, "Lord, help me!" Can you not read the heart's anguish in such a cry, as she continued knocking at a door that seemed to be closed against her?

Because God's blessings were for God's children, how could a worshiper of a heathen deity expect to share the same? Such appears to be the gist of our Lord's somewhat apparent harsh reply: "It is not meet to take the children's bread, and cast it to dogs." Jews were reckoned to be *children,* and salvation was theirs (John 4:22). Gentiles, however, were classed as *dogs* (Ps. 22:16; Matt. 7:6; Phil. 3:2; Rev. 22:15). But such a reply did not destroy the mother's hope so much as the fact of his replying increased it. Willingly, she owned that those of her nationality were as *dogs,* outsiders altogether, and without any claim upon mercy; but dogs get scraps, and what she desperately needed for her tormented child would not impoverish the *children* privileged to eat the rich food on the table. Like Jacob of old, the persistent mother wrestled with God in the flesh and prevailed. Deeply moved by her determination not to let him go, Jesus uttered one of the most remarkable sayings ever to leave his holy lips: "O woman, great is thy faith; be it unto thee even as thou wilt."

No longer silent, Jesus approves the boldness of the pleader, honors her faith, and grants her heart's desire in his last words to her. "There never has been a true prayer which did not somewhere, sometime, and in some shape, get completely answered." The Lord ever answers true, believing, and fervent prayer, if not in our way, then in his own way, which is ever the best way. For the Syrophoenician woman, the very letter of her request was granted. On reaching home, she found that her daughter was made whole the very moment Jesus uttered a commendable reply to her request.

This further miracle Jesus performed for a very needy child is additional proof that his presence was not necessary for the manifestation of his power. When he said to the anxious mother who would not take no for an answer, "Be it unto thee even as thou wilt," although there was considerable distance between the demon-possessed girl and Jesus, the miracle immediately happened. She was made whole and was resting calmly and comfortably on her bed when her mother returned. While it is true that "his *touch* has still its ancient power," it is likewise true that "his *thought* has still its ancient power"; no matter where we may be, he is able *to will* our relief in the hour of need.

The lunatic son (Matt. 17:14–21; Mark 9:14–29; Luke 9:37–43). The cry of the father in this incident is all the more bitter for this was his *only* child (Luke 9:38). For a full understanding of all that took place on this occasion, it is imperative to compare all the accounts of it found in the Gospels. Perhaps there are no other episodes in the ministry of Jesus so heavy with striking and instructive contrasts as those exhibited between the Mount of Transfiguration and the valley beneath. On the former there was *glory;* in the latter, *grief.* On the mount, *transfiguration;* in the valley, *tragedy.* On the mount, the three disciples wanted to bask in heavenly company forever; below, they miserably failed to assist Jesus and distressed souls. Instead of bringing the shining light of the mount into the darkness and despair of the valley, the disciples only added to the hopelessness of a panic-stricken heart among the multitude, as Matthew, Mark, and Luke narrate, Mark describing the situation with fullness.

But amid all the contrasts, there is the never-changing one, the outflashing of whose inherent glory Peter, James, and John had witnessed. The same compassion which brought Jesus down from heaven likewise constrained him to descend from the mount, with its conversation with glorified saints, to serve and save the sinful, suffering multitude in the valley below. Thus, vision and vocation are united, for what is the use of sublime spiritual experiences when "heaven comes down our souls to greet," unless they thrust us out into a world of suffering and sin to witness to the power of the crucified, glorified Christ to sympathize and save. May we be delivered from taking up the vocation without first having the vision!

1. *The miscellaneous multitude.* When Jesus came down from the mount with his three privileged disciples, he joined the other disciples left below, only to find them surrounded by a mixed multitude, among whom were the scribes and the father distressed about his demon-possessed child. That *great* multitude (Mark 9:14) revealed all the faults and better qualities of a crowd. There were curious scribes asking questions, and the depressed disciples asking theirs. Yet the majority of the multitude that day were "greatly amazed" when they beheld Jesus and, gathering around him, sa-

luted him. They hailed his arrival as if he had mysteriously appeared at the opportune moment to answer all questions and to bring to an anguished heart relief from a most tragic experience. Luke tells us that once Jesus performed the needed miracle, "they were all amazed at the mighty power of God. But . . . they wondered every one at all things which Jesus did" (Luke 9:43). But crowds can be fickle, as Jesus experienced when one day they shouted as he rode in triumph, *Hosanna!*—but almost the next day, *Crucify him!*

2. *The questioning queue.* When Jesus joined the large concourse of people, he found the scribes questioning the people, but what about we are not told. Doubtless these critics of his were abashed by his appearance, and meeting them he asked, "What question ye with them?" (Mark 9:16). Could it have been the same question that troubled the disciples, namely, their failure to cast out the dumb spirit causing the child so much pain and anguish? Evidently the disciples who were left behind in the valley when Jesus went up to the mount must have tried to rebuke the foul spirit possessing the boy in the presence of the people and the scribes before Jesus came on the scene. Seeing the helplessness of the disciples in the hour of need, the scribes probably debated with them over their failure and tried to confound them. "Error," says Barnes, "is always subtle, and often puts on the appearance of calm and honest inquiry."

What glorious results there might have been if only those critical, crafty scribes had encouraged the distressed disciples to persist in prayer for the lunatic child and had knelt down with the distraught father, joining the disciples in intercession to God for power to cast out the hellish spirit from his only child. In this way they could have prevented the failure they came to question and denounce, and argue that ill success in one case proves deception in all. As Richard Glover comments in *History of Jesus,* "Pity the woes of men, so often intensified and perpetuated by men disputing as to who is to blame for them, instead of uniting in the effort to cure."

3. *The pleading parent.* It is impossible to describe all the anguish of parental love behind the cry, "Master, I beseech thee, look upon my son: for he is mine only child"(Luke 9:38). The request was more intense because the father was pleading for his *only* child. If he died, the shadowed home would be without hope. Prostrate with grief, the father revealed reverence for the one whose help he sought for he "kneeled down to him." He likewise recognized the power of Jesus to meet the pressing need, for he called him, *Lord!* Thus high regard and earnest entreaty were combined. The prayer of the father was brief yet expressive of intense solicitude for his child he may have felt to be too hopeless a case to expect a cure. But he linked his despair and weakness in himself on to omnipotence and prevailed.

The extreme condition of the child added pathos to the parent's plea, for he was *lunatic,* or smitten with some form of insanity. He was *sore vexed,* meaning, the boy suffered greatly from his affliction. He *fell suddenly,* as persons do when overcome by an epileptic fit. He was *dumb,* except when a fit came upon him, for then *he suddenly cried out.* He *foamed and gnashed with his teeth,* that is, he convulsed, and *wasted away,* or became emaciated. *It tore him,* the demon-spirit bruising him, "hardly departed from him." *It hath cast him* into the fire and into the waters to destroy him. It was an *unclean spirit, foul spirit, dumb and deaf spirit, a devil,* or demon. What a terrible plight for a boy to endure. No wonder his father, whose anxious days and sleepless nights caring for his only child must have aged him, cried to Jesus, "If thou canst do any thing, have compassion on us, and help us."

4. *The sympathizing Savior.* Ever touched with the feeling of human infirmities, Jesus was deeply moved by the father's description of the terrible plight of his only child and also by the intensity of the parent's prayer for help. What immediately distressed the only one who could liberate the lunatic was the failure of his disciples to cast out the demon of hell, seeing he had delegated them power to perform such a miracle. Thus, his grief was mixed with sore displeasure that the disciples had caused both parent and child needless anguish. What a sting there was in the confession of the father, "I brought him to thy disciples, and *they could not cure him*" (Matt. 17:16). Do we realize that it is still a pain and a wound to Christ to see his church stand impotent and depressed amidst woes she might cure, if only she would stir up the power in her?

In his rebuke, Jesus used two words—*faithless* and *perverse.* The former was for the disciples whom the Master condemned with *unbelief* and lacking *faith as a grain of mustard seed.* The latter was for the questioning, critical scribes who, in their perverseness, prolonged the woes of the afflicted by their strife. How the troubles of the world today are accentuated by unbelief and perversity! But no disappointment could lessen the love of Jesus, and so there came his answer to the father's heartfelt cry as he met a human *if* with a divine *if*. *"If thou canst do* anything," was met with, *"If thou canst believe,* all things are possible to him that believeth" (Mark 9:22, 23).

In this reply, Jesus throws the burden of the situation back on the parent who, smitten with tears, cried out, "Lord, I believe: help thou mine unbelief." Here we have an honest and earnest confession, asserting faith, yet admitting unbelief and asking for a bigger blessing than his faith can hope for. There is an authoritative ring about our Lord's sweet invitation to the grief-stricken, exhausted father, *Bring him hither to me!* "Where the word of a king is, there is power" (Eccles. 8:4). Smitten and suffering from early childhood, the lad's case seemed hopeless, but none are beyond the king's power to liberate. The demon possessing the father's only child was rebuked in such a way as to cause the foul spirit to depart, and the child was cured from that very hour.

It will be noted, however, that there is a change of the divine healer's method here. In the two previous child-miracles, the presence of the healer was not necessary, nor were the sick brought to him. He healed them at a distance without seeing or speaking to them. But now Jesus commands the lunatic lad to be brought to him. Why? Can it be for the sake of the disciples who, failing to cast out the demon in the presence of the multitude, thereby lost the opportunity to reveal publicly what God was able to do through them? Perhaps Jesus asks for the presence of the afflicted child in order that the carping scribes and the people could witness what "the Son of God with power" was able to accomplish. All could see that he succeeded where others through unbelief had failed. In summarizing the lessons to be learned from this miracle of healing, Richard Glover has these guides:

1. There is no impotence in Christ, every woe of the human heart yields to His control.
2. Where He finds any faith, even as a grain of mustard seed, He can and will impart salvation.
3. When we fail, He will come and turn our failure into humility and victory.
4. There are many ills in life which, though physical, have their origin or their aggravation in the soul, and must find their relief or cure there.
5. There is no morbid condition of the body which the enemy will not take advantage of.
6. When Christ heals He works a permanent cure, saying, *Enter no more into him,* Mark 9:25. What gladness brought and still brings into the world! Let Him cast the evil out of your heart.
7. *Faith, Prayer, Fasting.* What the Church needs today to change her failure into success is, not a new creed, or new methods, or eloquence, or learning, or music but the three requisites of Faith, Intercession, and Fasting which make self-denial easier, and prevent indolence. With these, the *mountains* of drunkenness, of infidelity, of impurity, will remove at the Spirit-empowered Church's command.

Jairus' daughter (Matt. 9:18–26; Mark 5:22–45; Luke 8:41–56). The *little daughter* of this ruler, Mark tells us, was only *twelve years* of age. This account affords another illustration of the loving sympathy of Jesus for afflicted children. The miracle on this girl, the *only* daughter of Jairus, is unique in that it is a miracle wrapped up in another miracle. Following the ruler's request for Jesus to come to the house of gloom and lay his hands on his dying daughter, a woman with a twelve-year hemorrhage—the same length of time as the age of the girl Jesus was on his way to heal—hearing that the Great Physician was passing by, joined the crowd and, pressing close to him, touched his garment and was made whole. *His touch* brought life to a dead girl, but *the woman's touch* of him brought healing for her diseased body. In the narratives given by Matthew, Mark, and Luke, a miracle springs out of a miracle. The healing of the woman was a casual service performed on the road to another act of love and power. Before Jesus entered the house of Jairus, he accomplished a miracle on the way, and when he left the house, another miracle was experienced by the two blind men who cried to Jesus for mercy, and mercifully he restored their sight.

The raising of Jairus' daughter is another instance of home sorrow because of a child and of Jesus' power to banish grief and bring gladness to a shadowed household. How the Great Physician was in constant demand! There was never an hour in which he was not wanted for the work of love in which he was unceasingly active.

Resolve and reverence (Matt. 9:18; Mark 5:22, 23). Examining the miracle before us, we note first the attitude of Jairus himself as he approached Jesus with his intimation and invitation. "My daughter even now is dead: but come and lay thy hand upon her, and she shall live." The child was dying when her father left home, and he felt that by now she must be dead. As a ruler of the synagogue, Jairus held a responsible position and had heard the words of Jesus and witnessed his works. Therefore, he had no doubt as to Jesus' ability to raise his daughter from the dead. "Lay thy hand upon her, and she *shall* live." Coupled with his resolve to contact Jesus, in his desperate need, was his recognition of Jesus as one worthy to be reverenced, for coming into his presence, Jairus worshiped him. Mark and Luke tell us that "he fell at his feet" and "besought him that he would come into his house," but Jesus needed no urging to go to those in dire need of his assistance. With the chance that the girl was still alive, her father was eager for Jesus to come as quickly as possible.

Affliction quickens reverence and entreaty. The possibility of a great sorrow brought the ruler to his knees; he felt that if death claimed the child he dearly loved, everything would be changed in the home. A child is one of God's most precious and great gifts, one binding parents' hearts to each other. What would be your reaction *if* your child was taken from you? From Jairus we learn the power of sorrow to quicken faith and seek relief from one able to give it. Nothing is said about the dying girl's mother, whose anguish must have been deep. Jairus, who could not nurse as well as his wife, runs for the Savior. The mother who could not run so well, stays and nurses. Thus, they were workers together for the welfare of their dying child.

The petition Jairus presented to Jesus was the art of brevity—*only one sentence*—but that was sufficient. We are not heard for our much speaking. How much more effective our approach to the Lord would be if only we would take time to know what we actually need and then tell him in as few words as possible what is on our heart! Some of the greatest prayers in the Bible are the shortest. After all, did not Jesus himself teach that God knows what we have need of *before* we ask him? Then why waste breath and words on long prayers telling him what he already knows?

Response and rebuke (Matt. 9:19, 23, 24; Mark 5:24, 38–40). The response to the appeal of Jairus was immediate, for "Jesus arose, and followed him." How marvelous the compassion, the faith shown, in this promptitude of Jesus! This was the king's business and required haste. He had been discussing theological questions with his disciples, but these were quickly terminated for the cry of need. If you want to find Jesus still, you will more often come on his presence at the bedside of sufferers than in the books of scholars.

After an interruption on the way to the ruler's house, during which a woman who had spent all her money on doctors for relief from her issue of blood, without result, was completely healed, Jesus continued his journey. But he was met by a servant from the ruler's house who said to Jairus, "Thy daughter is dead: why troublest thou the master any further?" How crushed he must have been by such a bold statement! Jesus, when he heard of the needlessness of his help, did not turn round at the face of death but said to Jairus, "Be not afraid, only believe," which must have seemed a word of strange comfort. Yet it was a message preparing Jairus for a wonderful surprise.

Reaching the house, Jesus encountered a great

hullabaloo. Loud lamenting, tumult, and tears were much in evidence, similar in fashion to an old Irish wake. The howling for the dead and the inordinate, mournful sounds were mock grief, jarring the sorrowful occasion. These professional mourners could not comfort the parents in their loss by their *noise,* as Matthew puts it. Calming the tumult by his commanding presence, Jesus uttered the assuring announcement, "The damsel is not dead, but sleepeth." In the house, where the spoils of death were evident, he called death by the beautiful name *sleep.* Jesus did not deny that the girl was dead but denied that death is death in the sense of that hopeless separation the mourners felt. As quickly as they turned on their crocodile tears, the mourners turned them off, for they "*laughed* Jesus to scorn." As these scorners were not fit to witness his miracle-working power, "he put them all out."

Those whose mockery was out of harmony with the occasion scorned Jesus because they thought that he meant natural *sleep* when he used it as a symbol of death. It is contrary to his consistent teaching as to what happens after death, however, to assume that when a saint—or sinner, for that matter—dies, he or she remains unconscious until the resurrection of the dead. *Soul-sleep* is not a Scripture truth. When the figure is used in connection with death, it is always in connection with the body, never the soul (John 11:11, 14). Both Dives and Lazarus were conscious in their respective abodes *after* death (Luke 16:19–31). Paul assures us that the moment we depart from the body at death, we are immediately at home with the Lord.

Contact and command (Matt. 9:25, 26; Mark 5:40–43). Having expelled the callous weepers from the house, Jesus took the sorrow-stricken parents and Peter, James, and John into the room where the child was laid out, still and cold in death. They were privileged to witness him beard death in its den. They were to witness that the *dead* are living and can hear his voice although at home in the other world, and that he is the Lord of death, and it obeys him who is "the resurrection and the life." Life contacted death as Jesus took the damsel by the hand and said unto her *Talitha cumi,* meaning, "Damsel, I say unto thee, arise" or "Little one, get up!" perhaps words used daily by her mother to wake her.

As death could not keep its prey when it came to Christ's resurrection from the dead, so here, for as soon as he uttered the all-commanding word *arise,* "the maid arose." Jesus arose to journey to the house to meet her need (Matt. 9:19); now she arises to meet him. The child had not been spoiled for earth by her short visit to heaven but woke as if from a sweet dream to see the face of him who was able to deliver from the power of death, and the faces of her dear, astonished but delighted parents.

The impressive story closes on a most practical note. So real and complete was the girl's restoration to life that Jesus had wrought that she needed food. Jairus and his wife were too bewildered to think about food at such a time, but Jesus, intrinsically holy, was always intensely human and knew that health brings hunger; and so he "commanded that something should be given her to eat." How strange are the two precepts in succession—*Arise! Give her meat!* When the Savior himself rose again, he gave evidence of his own resurrection by eating with his disciples (John 21:1–13). Jesus raised Jairus' daughter by *extraordinary* power, but willed that she should be sustained by *ordinary* means. No wonder the fame of Jesus spread abroad in spite of his explicit wish that no man should know of what he had accomplished. How grateful we are that the first three evangelists recorded the miracle so that it has reached us through all the distance of time and space to comfort our hearts in sorrow and to strengthen our faith that one day all the dead in Christ shall rise again.

The widow's son (Luke 7:11–18). Although this is one of the most decisive and instructive of our Lord's miracles and resulted in his being a great prophet raised up by God, it is not actually within the scope of his contact with *children,* even though the one raised from the dead was the only son of his widowed mother. He is referred to as a *dead man,* and Jesus, who because of his omniscience knew all about him, called him a *young man*—probably about Jesus' own age. The resurrection of the children and of this young man and of Lazarus, who was somewhat elderly, prove that age makes no difference to Jesus when it comes to the manifestation of his power whether it be in physical resurrection or spiritual resurrection.

JESUS AND CHILDREN—TEACHINGS

Having considered many precious truths associated with our Lord's miraculous ministry among the children, let us now look at his direct teachings occasioned by the young as they crossed his pathway. How apt he was at using them as symbols of spiritual instruction which his disciples and others needed! That those around Jesus did not share his love, enthusiasm, and care for children comes through in a lesson he taught the disciples on the inclusion of the youngest in the divine plan. Devout mothers brought their infant children to Jesus that he might put his hands upon them and pray for them (Matt. 19:13–15; Mark 10:13–16; Luke 18:15–17). Often those who do not seek the Savior for themselves desire him for their children, but parents who are truly the Lord's know the surety he can afford their young ones when they are safe in his arms. If only more mothers and fathers had brought their children to Jesus to be blessed of him, we would not be faced with profligate youth so common today.

The disciples, with little time for children, and feeling that Jesus had no time for them, rebuked the parents for interrupting the Master in his busy life. Failing to understand his desire to welcome even infants to his heart, the disciples, insufficiently reverent to childhood, and thinking the mothers intrusive, felt that little children would not understand him and therefore should wait until they were older to receive his blessing. But the disciples' rebuke of the mothers earned the rebuke of the Master: "Suffer the little children, and forbid them not to come unto me; for of such is the kingdom of heaven."

The word *suffer* here means "do not hinder them" or "let them come." Phillips translates "forbid them not"—*you must never stop them.* "Let them alone," said Jesus. He welcomed the fresh faces and their innocent, artless smiles and rejoiced in the mothers' desire for him to bless their children and also in the attraction the young found in him. Jesus did not believe in letting the children go wrong and afterwards setting them right; he therefore welcomed them, weak though they were. It is better to build a strong barricade round the edge of a high cliff than to have an ambulance below. "Prevention is better than cure." Hence Jesus said, "Let them come unto me: for of such is the kingdom of heaven," or "the kingdom of heaven belongs to little children like these," as Phillips translates it. The kingdom includes a great multitude of children. In fact, only the childlike can enter the kingdom (Matt. 18:3). The children brought and blessed afford a strong contrast to the story that follows of the rich young ruler who, childlike, came to Jesus seeking a blessing but departed without it (Matt. 19:16–22; see Luke 18:17).

Jesus had already taught his disciples about God's interest in little children and that it was his desire that every child should be saved (Matt. 18:14) and that Jesus himself was their Savior (Matt. 18:10, 11). Knowing, therefore, how impressionable the child-mind is, and that childhood is a most convenient season for conversion and that a child enters the kingdom with ease, Jesus said, "Let them come unto me." Further, Jesus loves the little children because they are childlike and he can use them to make an entrance into other hearts for himself (Matt. 18:4–7). "A little child shall lead them" (Isa. 11:6). Once in the kingdom, they have his protection and the highest angels in heaven to guard them. Parents, teachers, and all workers among the young should share with the angels the sacred task of protecting them from the evil of the world (Matt. 18:10).

Mark gives us a beautiful glimpse of the Master's gratitude to the mothers for bringing their children to him: "He took them up in his arms, put his hands upon them, and blessed them" (Mark 10:16). In ancient Hebrew custom, this was a father's act, a blessing Esau sought from Jacob (Gen. 27:38). Bengel, the commentator, has the note on the benediction Jesus pronounced over the children of the mothers of Salem, "He had no children that he might adopt all children." He certainly charmed those young hearts to love him and is ever ready to fill with his love the little hearts that look up at his serene, smiling face. Richard Glover in his *History of Jesus* deals with Jesus' association with children:

> How Jesus likes children!—for their simplicity, Luke 18:17, their intuition, their teachableness, we say. But was it not, perhaps for far simpler and more natural reasons—just because they *were* children, and little, and delightful? We forget his little brothers and sisters, or we eliminate them for theological purposes.

What about your own children or those entrusted to your care? Have you brought them to Jesus to be saved and blessed by him? It should be our preeminent desire and effort to bring the young to him ere their precious lives are damaged by sin.

> Little children are remembered in the Saviour's promise,
> They may early share the blessings of redeeming grace:

He is watching kindly o'er them, and His word assures us,
That in Heaven their angels ever see the Father's face.

We have a further illustration of the Savior's interest in children and what can be learned from them when he had to rebuke his disciples for squabbling among themselves as to who should be the greatest among them. This episode gave Jesus the opportunity to teach his own—and us—a most precious lesson (Matt. 18:1–6; Mark 9:33–37; Luke 9:46–48), one that is very hard to take by those passed by all others for the chief seat at the feast. Mark's account describes the action of Jesus in taking a child out of the crowd and using him as a symbol of lowliness, of his identification with the child in humility, and of the necessity of caring for the child in his name. The Greek participle that Mark uses for "when he had taken him in his arms" (Mark 9:36; 10:16) actually means that Jesus was sitting with the little child on his knee and "in the crook of his arm." What a vivid and delightful glimpse this is of the loving way he nestled the child to his heart! Although we have instances of his happy way in dealing with children, we have no record of what he spoke to them about as they looked into each other's faces. Yet with them near to him, what important truths he taught others.

Jesus was "moved with indignation" at the way the disciples failed to realize the importance of children and of what can be learned from them (Mark 10:14). A little child is not only teachable, trustful, and loving, but also simple, unsophisticated, and free from mental pride. This was why

Jesus, as he nursed the child, reminded those around him that heaven is exclusively occupied by childlike people (Matt. 18:3). Those who want to be first strut around as if they owned the universe and court dislike because of their pomposity. They are not fit company for heaven where saints cast their crowns before him who is the first and the last.

Correcting the fleshy ambition of his disciples, Jesus teaches the importance of the child-spirit and that those lacking it needed to be *converted* and become as little children. The Savior speaks as if two conversions are necessary for our salvation; namely, one conversion *backward,* of the man into a child, and then a second conversion *forward,* of the childlike man into a Christian. Christ does not say, "Except children are converted into men" by flow of time, "they cannot enter the kingdom"; but, except men are converted into children, *they* cannot. Children have only to learn not to unlearn; only to do, not to undo. Ambition keeps men from entering; but children easily enter the kingdom.

What are some of the characteristics of this necessary conversion into the child-spirit Jesus emphasized?

Simplicity, acting on simplest grounds and from directest motives;

Freedom from self-consciousness, responsible for adult entanglement;

Deliverance from calculation, as to what others may say, or other days bring—children live in the present and are less overawed by the future;

Humility, or contentedness to be little and obscure if only loved. The secret of Christian greatness is the willingness to stoop, obey, love, forget self in others. *Humility,* like a child's, is the secret of *entrance* into the kingdom and *eminence* in it.

Lowliness within the heart permits the king to enter the heart. "Whoso shall receive one such little child receiveth me." We admit the Lord of glory to our souls when we give welcome to childlike lowliness instead of the pride of life. May ours be the "stainless peace of blest Humility," the poet wrote of! Jesus humbled himself and was among men as one that served; he left us an example that we should follow his steps.

> His life while here, as well as birth,
> Was but a check to pomp and mirth;
> And all man's greatness you may see
> Condemn'd by His humility.

Among the other references to children by Jesus, and teachings attached thereto, we have the *hosanna* of the children greeting him as he entered the Temple on the day of his entry into Jerusalem—hosannas which sorely displeased the chief priests and scribes who had no praise for Jesus. The hosannas of the crowd meant little to him, for he knew how quickly they could change to hate. Infant praises, however, greatly cheered his heart (Matt. 21:1–17). "Out of the mouth of babes and sucklings thou hast perfected praise." Those who loved the clink of money, received from the sale of doves for sacrifice, more than children singing praises to Jesus urged him to forbid their hosannas, but he only approved and invited them. Are you helping to gladden the Master's heart by teaching the children around you to praise him as the king of heaven?

How true it is that in old classical literature and in Christian literature of past ages no parallel can be found to the interest and joy Jesus found in children! His amazing love for the young can be traced in his lament over Jerusalem, in which he prophesied its coming disasters and paused to pity poor pregnant women and mothers with small babies in such perilous times (Matt. 24:19; Mark 13:14–23). Josephus reckons that in the destruction of Jerusalem in A.D. 70, over one million perished. (Consult the author's work, *All the Children of the Bible.*)

Jesus is also found using the term *children* as indicative of a relationship, in a figurative sense. Thus, he called the hypocritical Pharisees "children of hell" (Matt. 23:15; see Acts 13:10; 1 John 3:10). He addressed his own as "children" and "little children" (Mark 10:24; John 13:33; 21:5). Those whose lives are dominated by wisdom, he spoke of as "children of wisdom" (Matt. 11:19). Moral likeness or spiritual kinship is implied when he referred to those who claimed to be Abraham's seed as "children of Abraham" (John 8:39). What are we all if ours is a relationship based on regeneration but children! Tennyson asks in "In Memoriam":

> But what am I?
> An infant crying in the night;
> An infant crying for the light,
> And with no language but a cry.

Our final word is that we cannot meditate upon Christ's associations with children without realizing that all he taught concerning them forms the

Magna Carta for all parents and workers among the young. No efforts are more rewarding than those that are taken up with leading the lambs into his fold. Professor James Stalker says in *The Ethic of Jesus*:

> By the scene in which he blessed the little children he took possession forever of the heart not only of childhood but of motherhood; and it would be difficult to exaggerate the revolution in the condition of children and the estimation in which they are held which has been due to this incident alone. In all the centuries since, the words fall like leaven, and their virtue is not yet by any means exhausted.

Jesus had a keen sense of the value of the child and has taught us how children should be treated in the home and in society. The future of any country is in the hands of its children, a significant fact that must not be lost sight of in homelife, in our systems of education, and in all organizations concentrating upon childcare and welfare. Although there are still some parts of the world where Christ's estimate of the child is neither accepted theoretically nor applied in practice, for us in civilized lands his command still stands, "Bring the child to me" (Matt. 17:17).

BIBLE STUDY QUESTIONS

Take time to turn to each Scripture reference and mark the verse or a portion in your Bible.

1. Of what value and responsibility are children?

2. In healing the nobleman's son and Syro-phoenecian's daughter how did Jesus test and prove faith?

3. How was healing the lunatic son different from the previous two miracles?

4. How did Jesus show his concern and care for Jairus' daughter?

5. How did Jesus use children in his teaching?

Bibliography

Barnes, Albert. *Barnes' Notes on the New Testament.* Grand Rapids: Kregel Publications, n.d.

Bernard, T. D. *The Central Teaching of Jesus Christ.* London: Oxford Press, 1920.

Bond, A. R. *The Master Preacher.* New York: American Tract Society, 1910.

Dale, R. W. *Christian Doctrine.* London: Hodder & Stoughton, n.d.

Defoe, James. *Guide to Bible Study.* London: Society of Christian Knowledge, 1908.

———. *History of the Bible.* London: Gety, 1853.

Ellicott, Charles H. *Commentary on the Whole Bible.* Grand Rapids: Zondervan, 1951.

Fairbairn, A. M. *Studies in the Life of Christ.* London: Hodder & Stoughton, 1900. A spiritual treasure all Bible students should have.

Glover, Richard. *The Gospel of Matthew.* Grand Rapids: Zondervan, 1956.

———. *History of Jesus.* Grand Rapids: Zondervan, 1956.

Glover, T. R. *The Jesus of History.* London: Student Christian Movement, 1917.

Godet, F. *Godet's Commentary on the New Testament.* New York: Funk & Wagnalls, 1886.

Gore, Charles. *Jesus of Nazareth.* London: Thornton Butterworth Ltd., 1917.

Green, Peter. *Our Lord and Saviour.* London: Longmans, Green & Co., 1928.

Halley, Henry H. *Halley's Bible Handbook.* Grand Rapids: Zondervan, 1927.

Handbook of Christian Teaching. London: Sheldon Press, 1939.

Hastings, James. *Dictionary of the Bible.* Edinburgh: T. & T. Clark, 1909.

Hodgkin, Henry T. *Jesus among Men.* London: Student Christian Movement, 1930.

The International Standard Bible Encyclopedia. Grand Rapids: Wm. Erdmans, 1929. See articles on topics with which we have dealt.

Lange, John Peter. *Commentary on the Holy Scriptures.* New York: Scribner's, 1884.

Lee, Umphrey. *The Life of Christ.* Nashville: Cokesbury Press, 1926.

Liddon. H. B. *The Divinity of Our Lord.* London: Pickering & Inglis, 1864.

Lockyer, Herbert. *All the Children of the Bible.* Grand Rapids: Zondervan, 1970.

———. *All the Miracles of the Bible.* Grand Rapids: Zondervan, 1961.

———. *All the Parables of the Bible.* Grand Rapids: Zondervan, 1963.

Macartney, Clarence E. *What Jesus Really Taught.* Nashville: Abingdon Press, 1958.

Mackintosh, H. R. *The Doctrine of the Person of Christ.* International Theological Library. New York: Scribner's, 1912.

Morgan, G. Campbell. *The Teaching of Christ.* London: Marshall, Morgan, & Scott, 1930.

Moorehead, W. E. *Old and New Testament Outline Studies.* New York: Revell, 1893.

Patterson, W. P. *Christ and the Gospels.* Edinburgh: T. & T. Clark, 1911.

Pierson, A. T. *Knowing the Scriptures.* London: James Nisbet Co., 1910.

Scroggie, W. Graham. *A Guide to the Gospels*. London: Pickering & Inglis, 1948.

Stalker, James. *The Christology of Jesus*. London: Hodder & Stoughton, 1899.

———. *The Ethic of Jesus*. London: Hodder & Stoughton, 1919.

Vincent, Marvin R. *Word Studies in the New Testament*. New York: Scribner's, 1882.

Warfield, Benjamin B. *The Lord of Glory*. London: Hodder & Stoughton, 1909.

Wescott, B. F. *The Gospels*. Edinburgh: T. & T. Clark, 1884.

Whyte, Alexander. *The Walk, Conversation, and Character of Jesus Christ Our Lord*. London: Oliphant, n.d.